MW01226794

You Can Do Anything:

A Guide to Success, Motivation, Passion and Laughter

Library and Archives Canada Cataloguing in Publication

Cherniak, Boris, author
You can do anything : a guide to success, motivation, passion and laughter
/ Boris Cherniak.

Issued in print, electronic and audiobook formats.
ISBN 978-0-9687994-3-7 (hardback).
ISBN 978-0-9687994-4-4 (paperback).
ISBN 978-0-9687994-7-5 (pdf).
ISBN 978-0-9687994-5-1 (html).
ISBN 978-0-9687994-6-8 (audiobook)

1. Cherniak, Boris. 2. Self-actualization (Psychology). 3. Success.
4. Hypnotists--Canada--Biography. 5. Entertainers--Canada--Biography.
6. Comedians--Canada--Biography. I. Title.

BF1127.C44A3 2016   792.02'8092   C2016-901469-X
                                                 C2016-901470-3
                                                 C2016-901471-1

You Can Do Anything: A Guide to Success,
Motivation, Passion and Laughter

©Boris Cherniak 2016

All rights reserved. No part of this book may be reproduced or transmitted in any form or by any means, electronic or mechanical, including photocopying, recording, or by an information storage and retrieval system – except by a reviewer who may quote brief passages in a review to be printed in a magazine, newspaper, or on the Web – without permission in writing from the author.

Cover Design by Kimma Parish
Book & Back Cover Design by Nikki Ward, Morrison Alley Design

First Printing 2016

Although the author and publisher have made every effort to ensure that the information in this book was correct at press time, the author and publisher do not assume and hereby disclaim any liability to any party for any loss, damage, or disruption caused by errors or omissions, whether such errors or omissions result from negligence, accident, or any other cause.

I have tried to re-create events, locales, and conversations from my memories of them. In order to maintain their anonymity, in some instances I have changed the names of individuals and places, and I may have changed some identifying characteristics and details such as physical properties, occupations, and places of residence.

ISBN 978-0-9687994-4-4

For Sophia, Julia, Daphna, my parents and YOU

Table of Contents

"Be so good they can't ignore you."

- Steve Martin

Preface

This is a book about choices and decisions. As a student of psychology, I learned that humans are genetically programmed to fear the worst. And yet, life teaches us that *we* are the only ones who can actually put limitations on our thinking and actions. Too often, we behave in a way that shows we are afraid of a myriad of possible negative results, instead of focusing on the limitless opportunities.

As a comedian, I have trained myself to see the funnier side of the world. The odd, quirky, and out of the ordinary are what make me laugh. I figured out early on that it is easier for me to learn while I am having fun. I think that is true for most people. Television commercials are more memorable when they are directed at your funny bone, online videos go viral when people laugh and share them with friends and family, and presentations are a big hit when they include a few chuckles.

With that in mind, I am going to do my best to both educate and inform you. I have written the pages you are about to read partially because I have a few things to get off my chest, but also because I want to deliver a message. By sharing some stories, examples, and setbacks from my own life, I hope to show you some of the powerful lessons I have learned.

People often ask me how I have managed to make it in a tough business, appearing on many television shows and speaking to hundreds of audiences every year. The short answer boils down to one thing: While others talked about doing, *I did*. While others described the world, I experienced it in my travels and soaked it in.

Along the way, I had many failures. These setbacks were used as stepping stones, and taught me that failure is sometimes an important ingredient of success. If you attempt something bold, you *will* fail, and more than once. But, you can use every failure as a learning tool. Then, you can devise a course of action that will move you to come out on top and exceed your own expectations. You will approach every task with a fearless attitude, knowing that shortcomings will only make you stronger.

As you read those words, I want you to have an "aha" moment that leads you to soar in your own capabilities.

Fear limits possibilities. To be successful, you have to learn to decipher situations as they present themselves. You must use logic to understand what you are doing, both right and wrong, and then adjust your course in life. That is really the secret to success in my business or any other. You must act, eliminating and eradicating your fears along the way. Most of what we are afraid of is unknown, and much of it will never come true. Once you get over your fears, you stop limiting your own growth.

A reporter once described me as someone who speaks in sound bites. As a well-known comedian and troublemaker, I take that as a compliment. My brain loves to draw comparisons, and my profession has taught me to use those metaphors to help translate ideas to others. My big hope, with this book, is that I can use my recollections and insights to cause you to act. As a hypnotist, I provide suggestions that lead to positive results. That can happen on a stage, within a private coaching session, or through a printed page.

If you read on, I promise you will find some advice that can change your life. You will also get a few laughs, and learn the answer to some interesting questions, such as: How does a boy from Moscow become an internationally known comic? What does it mean to be an "Alien of Extraordinary Abilities"? And, did I hypnotize my wife to fall in love with me?

Boris Cherniak

Boris: The Pre-Incredible Years

You may know me as the Incredible Boris. I love that adjective: *incredible*. It gives the sense of extraordinary things that can be done on stage, but also a clue toward the way I think we should all lead our lives. As hard as it might be to believe, however, I was not born as the Incredible Boris. In fact, my life took more than a few twists and turns along the way. Let's start at the very beginning…

I was born on December 12, 1964, in Moscow. I had a normal, happy childhood, with parents who loved me dearly and provided me with everything they could within their means (which admittedly was not much).

I am part of a large family. My father, Michael, was the youngest of five children. He had two older brothers, who in turn each had children and grandchildren of their own. He also had an adopted brother and sister. My grandmother took them into her house, and raised them as her own, after Nazis killed their parents before their eyes. That is why, to this day, I have a soft place in my heart for soldiers, and anyone who protects peace.

On the other side of my family, my mother, Galina, had two sisters. Her father disappeared without a trace during World War II. Her mother eventually remarried, and my great-grandmother took care of raising her.

My father worked as a hairstylist, supporting his family from the time he turned 16 years old. His hard-working spirit was instilled within me at an early age. He also happens to be one of the funniest people I have ever known. My mother, on the other hand, is a tough cookie. She is strict, but fair. She has a master's degree in electrical engineering, and was always the one to help me with my homework. She instilled the logical thinking process I used to turn my dreams into reality.

I can still remember her teaching me to play chess, and then using the experience to show me how important it was to approach every task decisively. Time helps determine solutions. However, dwelling on a problem inhibits clear thinking. "The more you stare at a problem," she explained to me, "the more out of focus things become." That was one of the most important lessons I ever picked up about life that I hope to pass on to you in the coming chapters.

I believe that I picked up the best traits of both of my parents' personalities. From my father, I learned to stand up for myself while having fun and enjoying every day. My mother taught me the importance of being warm and loving, but also that decisive action and forward movement are the key ingredients to a successful life.

Rather than go on and on about their virtues, I think I can best explain the values my family gave me with a few short stories and experiences from my childhood…

I was a small kid, usually the smallest in my class. In gym, when we lined up according to height, I was always the last one in line. I grew later, but at the time, my size allowed others to bully me mercilessly. I figured out pretty quickly that bullies normally picked on people who were alone and defenseless, rather than being part of a group. So, I learned how to make friends quickly and easily.

I also learned that there is more than one way to deal with a difficult situation. One day, a bigger kid beat me up, and I came home crying after school. My dad, being the protective man he was, took me back the next day and threatened the kid himself. My father never laid a hand on him – he only used words. Because of that talk, the bully never approached me again.

Heading home after the encounter, my dad kept me laughing. I cannot remember the jokes he told, but I was definitely impressed by the way a tough situation could be diffused with humor. My dad is still one of the funniest people I know, and always takes a lighthearted approach to life. He took what could have been a terrible, difficult moment, and had me laughing hysterically. The example he set has been invaluable to me and will be for the rest of my life.

We Are All the Same

Moscow was a busy and bustling city, full of people from all walks of life. The only time anyone ever stopped was to wait in line for groceries or sales items. Lines were a regular occurrence – store shelves advertised products in empty boxes, even though the items were not available for purchase. When merchandise eventually *was* delivered to the store, huge lines formed instantly. Demand exceeded the supply. People lined up even without knowing what they were going to buy, once word spread that a shipment was in. People regularly lined up in order to get meat, dry goods, even toilet paper. Yes, toilet paper was a luxury. When it ran out, it was replaced with newspapers ripped into squares.

It was in one of those lines that I first saw a man who was different than any I had ever laid eyes on before. He was tall, and good-looking, but what I really noticed was that his skin was dark. Before that moment, I had never seen anyone like him before.

With the innocence that can only come from a child, I walked over to him and rubbed his hand to see if the color came off. Luckily, he understood what I was doing, and took the time to bend down and explain to me (with incredible patience) that he was different from me only by the color of his skin. He had been born that way, just as I had been born with my own skin color.

That day I learned to like and judge people for what they have on the inside, not for the superficial differences. Instead of being troubled by "culture shock," I try to seek it out. I love engaging in conversations with people who come from different places or backgrounds, comparing their "normal" to my "different." My parents both showed this kind of open spirit in the way they met and shared with others, and I know that it rubbed off on me.

A Question of Integrity

Both my parents always taught me that it is important to do what is right and be consistent with your own morals. Once, during a grade school test in Russia, I discovered I had forgotten to bring an eraser. I carefully wrote my answers on the test paper until I had run out of room.

Still, I had more answers than available space. When I turned to ask a friend to borrow his eraser, my teacher noticed and accused me of trying to cheat. I was indignant – I had known the answers and cheating was the furthest thing from my mind!

I defended my actions and my innocence. My teacher did not believe me, and told me to leave the class and wait in the hallway until everyone else had finished their exam. I refused. In my mind, I had not done anything wrong, and did not feel a punishment was deserved.

A few of my classmates offered to help the teacher by forcibly removing me, and the whole fiasco ended like a routine from *Benny Hill* or *Scooby Doo*, with a number of people chasing me around the classroom while I dodged them. The test was completely disrupted, and as you can imagine, my instructor was not pleased. My parents were called into the school to discuss the situation, but I was never scolded for my actions. In the end, they praised me for standing up for myself and doing what was right. In their minds, that was the real lesson to be learned.

Comedic Instincts

My parents kept a modest home, barely making ends meet. We shared a two-bedroom apartment with another family in the center of Moscow.

Each family occupied a single bedroom, while the kitchen and washroom were used as a common space.

Everything in our one room was foldable – it had to be, because the space was only fourteen square meters. For example, my parents' bed was a divan that stored sheets and pillows in a compartment underneath during the day. The cover of our linen chest transformed into a table. It had two holes instead of handles, and foldable legs that could adjust to the necessary height. A futon became my bed at night. It was positioned next to a lacquered armoire.

Because of this limited space, my parents watched television just a few feet from where I slept. In fact, when I was sent to bed, they told me to turn around, face the wall, and go to sleep. Usually, I watched the reflection of the television on the shiny armoire wall until I fell asleep. And so, from an early age I developed great peripheral vision, along with an uncanny sense of what it took to become a performer. Even if I could not *see* what was going on, I could *hear* it and see flickers of the images bouncing before my eyes.

We lived in that small apartment in downtown Moscow until my brother, Alex, was born. I was nine years old at the time, and absolutely adored him. It was great to suddenly have another human being around that I could relate to. I became his guardian while my parents were at work, and learned how to do simple things like cook so I could take care of us both.

I also learned how to occupy my time by utilizing my imagination. Even though I could get glimmers of inspiration from the television, there were only a few channels that were available at night. Most of my playtime during the day, taken from spare moments while my brother was occupied, was spent on reading. I have always had an insatiable curiosity and a great need for information. It was during this point in my life I learned that I could consume books to satisfy that need.

Because my parents were often at work, I became independent at an early age. In fact, I used to take the bus around town to go visit my father's mother, Sophia.

In those days, the buses had intercoms with drivers announcing the stops. Because I traveled the same route regularly, I got to know both the drivers and the stops. And so, it came about that the drivers let the "friendly kid" they saw regularly call out some of the stops as a way to pass the time.

Being the budding comedian, I started adding a little bit of extra comical commentary to the route. For instance, when describing an upcoming bus stop, I announced: "Beer factory. Winos and drunks, please exit now." I was able to get a laugh from the other passengers, and started to realize my wit and sense of humor might be my best qualities.

Grandma Sophia was an incredibly interesting woman. She was small in stature, but tough as nails, and with a giant heart. I was a creative kid who loved drawing. When I ran out of paper, I scribbled on the wallpaper in her one-room apartment. Even though I covered most of her walls with pictures and writings, she never complained once, or even replaced the wallpaper.

Next to her house was a supermarket where fish were sold from a tank. You could walk in and buy fresh carp to cook for the night's meal. The fish was so fresh, in fact, it arrived home wrapped in a newspaper, still alive and wriggling. When it was ready to be cooked, my grandmother whacked it with a rolling pin and got to work.

I have always been a bleeding heart. One day, when my grandmother was running errands, she left a still-wriggling fish on the kitchen table. I remember filling the bathtub with water and setting it loose within to swim and be free until it was ready to be eaten.

When my grandmother Sophia returned home, I expected her to scream at me. Instead, she simply hugged me with tears in her eyes. Even though she had a tough life, and shared the same logical approach to the world that my mother did, she taught me that there is always room in the world for warmth and compassion.

Looking back, I think I reminded my grandmother of her husband – my grandfather Haim – who was never around. As a child, I was told by my parents and relatives that he was working far away, and was going to return with many presents for me someday. Beyond that, the topic was always brushed aside.

I patiently awaited his return and those gifts. It was not until later I learned that he had spent thirteen years in jail for helping to distribute clothes for the poor. Eventually, he was released due to poor health, and died nine months later.

My parents never told me about this. I only learned about it when I overheard them speaking to a relative, not realizing I was in the room. Before he passed, my grandfather told my dad that if he wanted a better life for us kids, he needed to head west to America or Canada. My father took this advice to heart, gathered the family and moved abroad.

At the time, you could only make such a move if you were sponsored by a relative in the destination country. It was a difficult, time-consuming process that was not guaranteed to bring any success. But my mother has an iron will. Once she had decided it was the right move for our family, it was only a matter of time before it happened.

With a course being set to move from Russia to the west, and my comedic instincts starting to take root, all the ingredients for a life full of adventure were starting to fall into place…

The Moscow Circus

In the center of Moscow was a magical building I visited at every available opportunity – The Moscow Circus.

I *loved* being there. As a child, everything about it felt magical. Unlike today's traveling shows, it was a full-time circus with everything from trained animals to acrobats, and even a carnival barker. Although there were plenty of attractions to choose from, what engaged my attention the most were the clowns. In between the other acts, they kept the show moving and provided laughter with slapstick skits. I loved their ability to put smiles on the faces of audience members.

The atmosphere was like what you'd find in the theater today, with serious, dedicated performers who were often greeted with flowers after a great show. In fact, there were vendors with stalls around the circus where you could buy bouquets if you wanted to give one personally.

I regularly used my small allowance to do so, and as a result came to be friendly with Yuri Nikulin and Oleg Popov, who were two of Russia's finest clowns of the time. I was at the circus so often they began to recognize me and call me by my name.

Yuri, in particular, made a huge impression on me. I spoke to him for what seemed like hours at a time while he removed his makeup after shows. To this day, his personalized autographed – complete with a few scribbled words of encouragement on a playbill – is one of my prized possessions.

I wanted to be just like him. In my mind, making another person laugh was the greatest feeling and gift you can give to them. Even though the performances and speeches I give are different than the ones I saw from him so many years ago, I am incredibly grateful for the time he and Oleg spent with me, and the lasting impression they made.

My Mother's Cultural Attaché

My parents were constantly working in order to stay afloat. I like to think their incredible work ethic was passed along to me, both genetically and through the example they set, which is why I was able to find my way to the top in the very competitive world of show business.

Even though we did not have a lot of money, my parents always made a point to enrich me culturally as much as possible. My mother, in particular, often took me to see interesting shows and exhibits as her companion. We attended museums, theaters, and events she considered informative.

I was her date for ballet and the theater, considering the King Tut exhibit one month and works by prestigious painters and sculptors the next. Although I did not fully appreciate the artistry or historical importance behind those great works at the time, I took them in with great enthusiasm. I really enjoyed being my mother's cultural attaché.

I remember on one occasion an electronics show came to town. My mother brought me along in the hopes that it would prove to be an educational experience. Many of the exhibits were hands-on, and all of the ideas seemed well ahead of their time. I got a joyful kick from playing with futuristic gadgets.

One demonstration that really made an impression on me was a video telephone. It was two black-and-white television screens that each had a built-in camera, microphone, and speaker. Long wires stretched into an adjoining room where another screen was connected through a similar setup, with a glass wall separating the users. Amazingly, you were able to have a conversation with someone on the other end.

This seemed incredibly forward thinking, given that telephones could only carry voices at the time. Still, the presenters insisted it was very possible for every household to have this technology in the future.

On the bus ride home, my mother and I had a long discussion about the concept, and when it might actually become available. Lo and behold, today we easily communicate with laptops or smartphones in the palm of our hand, and even do it wirelessly.

The way technology changes is amazing, and often exceeds our expectations. I learned from an early age to become a forward thinker. The habit of welcoming what is new and different has stopped me from being "stuck" when so many others have clung to old ways and ideas. Embrace innovation – you will have a much easier time getting to the top and staying there.

The Value of a Great Teacher

My first introduction to the English language was through a teacher I had in grade school. He had recently returned from working in India, and was fluent in both English and Russian. His teaching method involved having students memorize poems that emphasized proper pronunciation, and then working on them through constant repetition. To this day, I still find myself thinking of "Solomon Grundy, born on Monday, married on Tuesday…"

I took to English quickly, and served as my family's translator in our later travels. But perhaps even more valuable than the language skills I picked up were the lessons I got from being around a good instructor who was passionate about his subject.

In my life, I have come to appreciate that there is no such thing as a bad student; there is only a teacher who has not found the right approach. I was always hungry for new information and ideas, and found myself drawn to teachers who recognized my curiosity. In doing so, they were able to make difficult subjects fun. When you enjoy what you are doing, learning gets a lot easier. That is probably why the teachers I had in music, computers, and psychology all stood out in my mind.

We should always remember that in the same way a great teacher can inspire you, so too can a poor one. I have been lucky enough to mostly work with great instructors and coaches, but the few that were less patient or understanding helped to drive me in their own way.

In tenth grade, for instance, I had a teacher who constantly berated me. Most of us have had a teacher we think of as a "witch," and she was certainly mine. She almost seemed to take delight when I got things wrong. And, even though my English skills were excellent for someone picking up the language on the fly, she did not appreciate it when I misunderstood something or asked extra questions after class.

One day, she even suggested I was better suited for a remedial English course for immigrants. I found the comment hurtful, given all the time I had put into learning vocabulary and pronunciation. Instead of letting her persuade me to lower my own expectations, I worked twice as hard to ensure I could speak, understand, and be understood as well as anyone else. I used a negative to create a positive force to drive my ambitions by not allowing them to deviate me from my path to success.

Today, I use the English language for a living. My words entertain, transform thinking patterns, and sometimes even change lives. That has only been possible because I got the help I needed from some great teachers in my life… and figured out how to use the bad ones for extra motivation.

Mr. Show Biz

If you believe in fate or destiny, then you will understand that I was always going to become an entertainer. It is not just that I want to make others laugh, it is that I *have* to. It is part of what I do and who I have become.

Although I have now been performing professionally for more than half my life, and have been on stage in many different roles and disciplines – from theater to music to comedy – the love of whipping an audience into a delightful frenzy came to me even earlier.

It was not a conscious decision. But, just like moths are drawn to flames, I was pulled to the stage. Even as a young kid, I was very fond of comedians. Back in those days, their routines were recorded albums that I listened to over and over. Not only did I memorize the jokes they told, but also the tone, inflection, and delivery with which the bits were delivered. In fact, I listened to them so much, and ingrained them so deeply into my memory, that I still remember many of those old standup performances today.

This early comedic training often came out at family gatherings. Because I had many aunts, uncles, and cousins, there were regular occasions for us to get together at events like simple "family nights," holidays and birthday parties.

These were always joyful reunions. In the grand Russian tradition of making guests feel welcome, tables overflowed with food and drink. The noise from dozens of us meeting together, laughing and telling stories, was almost deafening.

Following an elaborate meal, there was always a show. The adults sat in a circle while the kids provided entertainment. Some kids danced or sang, but I liked to do impressions. I gave exaggerated impersonations of different individuals, accentuating the punchlines by pulling faces. I got to be so good at this, at such an early age, that I was told my impressions were really *impressions of impressions* because they were so spot on.

Family members loved my enthusiasm, and laughter became the drug I craved most. So, as I developed a knack for comedy, I took on the unofficial role of host and master of ceremonies for the family get-togethers. I greeted guests at the door, or sometimes delivered elaborate toasts with a champagne flute filled with apple juice.

I remember on one such occasion, I snatched a glass from the table and raised it in the air with the force of someone committed to delivering the best and most meaningful toast ever. Unfortunately, the fragile champagne flute snapped in half. The base and stem remained on the table, while the part that held the liquid flew into the air, soaking several guests.

Even though the champagne flute was made of expensive crystal, no one scolded me. Instead, everyone started laughing at the unexpected bit of slapstick. The words I had planned to deliver in that toast have long been forgotten, but I still smile thinking of the merriment that came from that moment now, even so many years later. That was perhaps my first and most powerful introduction to the art of improvisation. A good performer has to learn to roll with the punches, which is a lesson that has served me well everywhere I have performed, whether it has been a Russian dinner table or a packed comedy club.

A more formal (and unexpected) introduction into show business came not long after. My school was having a talent show, and I had been planning to tell a few jokes. At one point in the proceedings, however, a teacher noticed the next group was not ready with their costumes. So she handed me the microphone and instructed me to buy some time.

"Stretch" is a theater term that means to stall and fill time on stage. Unfortunately, it was not until many years later that someone explained this idea to me. On that night, my teacher pushed me through the slit in a heavy curtain and I found myself standing in the spotlight, armed only with a few jokes and my instincts.

Fortunately, I have always been a quick thinker and steady under pressure. So I slipped into the character who had delivered so many comedy bits at family functions in the past. Then, I started running through the standup routines I had memorized from my records, delivering them as if they had been written specifically for me.

Time seemed to stretch on forever as the audience listened in polite silence. It was likely no more than a few seconds after I delivered my first punch line, but it felt like that instant was never going to end. Then, a few chuckles were followed by roaring laughter, which spread contagiously from one person to another like a bolt of lightning.

I stole the show that night, and earning the laughter of a bigger audience gave me a surge of adrenaline like nothing I had ever experienced before. It is the same feeling that drives me forward to this day, and something that still gives me a deep sense of joy and fulfillment.

Any of us can become what we were meant to be, if we are only willing to practice, follow our passion, and take the chances we get to stand out when opportunities present themselves. Often, that is when we find out what we are really capable of.

Citizens of No Country

To leave Russia in the 1970s was very difficult. You had to be sponsored by someone outside the country, and then prove to the Russian government that you had a place to go.

My family is Jewish. My mother had a distant aunt, Betty, who lived in Israel and was able to provide us with the necessary sponsorship papers. My parents had planned to apply to leave Russia early in 1976, but delayed the application when I broke my leg while playing on ice with a friend one sunny winter day. My clumsiness could have nearly cost us our chance at a new life.

Luckily, things worked out and our papers were filed with the government a year later. What followed was a very difficult and uncertain time. We were unsure whether we would get approved to depart or have our request refused, but kept this anxiety to ourselves. If our application was refused, we could be persecuted as outcasts, or even traitors, for wanting to leave "Mother Russia."

My mother and father wanted desperately to find new opportunities. But they *also* wanted to ensure no one found out about their intentions.

On April 21, 1977, my parents received word that we were allowed to leave. We were given only two weeks to get our affairs in order, denounce our citizenships, pack our belongings, and ship our furniture by boat before we could depart the country. With visas that identified us as immigrants, we boarded a plane to Vienna, Austria. For the next year, we officially traveled as citizens of no country.

Upon arriving in Vienna, my first memory is of seeing glass doors at the airport that opened and closed on their own. I had never witnessed such an amazing novelty. While my parents gathered our luggage, I spent a great amount of time experimenting and trying to find out how close I could get to the door without it noticing my movements.

The only other memories I have of Vienna are of collecting our belongings and being ushered along with the other arriving immigrants to a waiting area. From there, we were transported to holding quarters by a team of armed soldiers in a convoy. After a very long drive, we arrived at a gated compound with even more armed guards.

There was a strange mixture of excitement and uncertainty, and the next few days flew by in a haze. Before I knew it, though, we departed Vienna and boarded a plane to Israel.

When we arrived, it was a hot summer day. Our family was issued papers to head to an "ulpan," which is a place where the "alé hadash" (meaning the newly arrived) could stay. We were sent to Atlit, a small town outside Haifa, where our new living quarters were to be situated.

It looked as if we were going to start a new chapter for the Cherniak family. My brother and I were going to learn Hebrew as our new language, and my parents were excited to find work and put down roots for their future.

However, it did not take long for plans to change. When you are immigrating, there is always the option to move on, given that you do not have anything holding you to one particular place. My parents went to Israel because they were committed to finding a better life for their kids, but quickly determined they were not going to find the kind of future they had envisioned in that place.

I was not privy to all that happened, and was too young to really comprehend the full extent of our situation. But I know from what my parents have told me in the years since that work and money were both very scarce. Both my mother and father had trouble finding steady employment, and, proud as they were, did not want to live off of government assistance.

So, just four months after our immigration, they made the difficult choice to head farther west. This time, we could not leave together as a family. My mother departed immediately with my brother and me, while my father stayed behind to sell our belongings (which still had not arrived from Russia) so he could scrape together enough money to join us and pay our bills. It was the only way we were able to afford another chance.

Separation Anxiety

In the end, my mother, brother and I left for Athens, Greece. It was four long months before we would see my father again.

Our time in Greece was relatively short, lasting only eight months. But it made a big impression on me for a number of reasons. In fact, I had already started seeing a whole new world of possibilities on the cab ride from the airport to our hotel.

The taxi was very cramped. In addition to my mother, my brother, and myself, there were two American women, plus our driver, in a very small vehicle. But it was a long ride, and I was finally able to display my knowledge of and proficiency with the English language to a pair of native speakers. The ladies we shared a cab with were very talkative, and took pleasure in discussing anything and everything under the sun. They asked me if I collected coins, and presented me with a U.S. silver dollar as a memento of our meeting.

That dollar meant more than they will ever know. It fueled my curiosity and gave me the courage to start speaking in a new language to strangers. It also sparked an interest in coin collecting as a hobby.

When we finally arrived, it was at a hotel that served as a housing place for immigrants who were waiting to be accepted into a new country. We were poor and without a home, but so was everyone else around us.

It was fortunate that we were already used to living in small quarters, because the hotel was very cramped. We were not allowed to cook in the room, but my mother found a hot plate and secretly made soups every day in an effort to save the little money we had. I can still remember how every time she cooked she opened the windows to make sure the smell did not creep into the hallway. There was not any refrigeration, so she boiled our meals several times a day to make sure the stock did not spoil. We might have only had soup to eat for eight months straight, had the hotel not provided us with breakfast. We were always sure to get up and be fed on time, and to discreetly stock up on jams, condiments, and buns for later meals.

At night, we watched television in the hotel's common room. The space also doubled as a restaurant, but was typically empty after the dinner rush. I loved to watch Western shows in English. That was a good thing, because there were no other choices. The TV was on a platform, and was set to a single channel that could not be changed. And so, I was exposed to fine programming like *Charlie's Angels*, *Carol Burnett*, and *The Six Million Dollar Man*. Beyond entertaining me, each of these characters unknowingly served as my personal English language tutor.

Local Customs

During the day, I ventured around the city with my brother. We learned little bits of the Greek language, and big bits of life and human nature. For the first few weeks we walked the streets aimlessly. Greeks love children in general, and my brother was adorable. Strangers often bought small chocolates for him from the newsstands you could find on every corner. He shared these sweets with me, and in this way we were able to sample treats we could never have afforded on our own.

After a while, we figured out that children could get into museums for free. And so, we spent a lot of time marveling at the masterpieces displayed in these houses of art and history. Because we did not have any mode of transportation, we walked *everywhere*. We visited parks and historical landmarks – like the Parthenon and public squares filled with pigeons that flew and sat on your hands and head when offered bread crumbs. We let our feet take us where they will, while still paying attention.

At noon, we could witness the change of the guard – men in military white dress and huge pointy wooden shoes with colorful woolen pompoms ceremoniously walked in unison to change places with their counterparts in a special marching step that makes them look like they are dancing. I have fond memories of my brother and me running next to that procession. Once they were in place at their post, we tried to make those soldiers laugh. But they never talked, blinked, or even smiled, no matter what we did.

I also figured out that many situations in life are governed by unwritten rules or customs. For instance, my brother and I were especially fond of an arcade near our hotel that featured bumper cars. What boy does not love an attraction that involves crashing into others at speed with destructive force?

Even though we did not have any money to use the bumper cars, I used to stare at them longingly. I was happy to simply watch. Over time, I realized each car had a large number painted on it, and some of the numbers were read over the loudspeaker after each session had ended. I had learned the words for the numbers in Greek by helping my mother to negotiate for groceries at the market.

By studying this phenomenon for a while, I came to realize why these numbers were so important: The proprietors of the bumper car business made their money from selling tokens to tourists. However, there were not enough tourists at all hours of the day to keep the bumper car track busy, and no one would pay to ride if there were no others to crash into. And so, they called out the numbers of cars that could be ridden by locals for free before the next race began.

The difference between paying to use the bumper cars and riding them for free was a simple matter of knowing where to look and what to listen for. Better yet, if the attendants got to know you, they often gave you a wink and slid a magic token into the car you were using even if the number was not called.

So many things in life are like that. Once you understand how the game you are playing works, and form the right relationships, you are able to do what other people cannot or will not. There is a lot of power in being knowledgeable and observant, and being friendly with the right gatekeepers. Those insights paid big dividends in my comedy career.

Moving Forward

Overall, the eight months we spent in Greece were a happy and busy time in my life. I became more independent and self-sufficient. I learned how to entertain myself without needing money. I read books, did homework, and improved my English language skills by watching television. Much of this was done out of necessity. My mother's primary concern was to keep us fed and clean on something less than a shoestring budget, all while regularly visiting the offices of consulates and organizations that could help us move to North America.

And yet, even though my memories of Athens are positive, it was also a very uncertain time for our family. As the months stretched on, there was a strong possibility that my mother would have to move us along to a new country without my father. We did not have the money to stay indefinitely, and would need to depart quickly if offered the chance. We tried not to think about this potential outcome, even though my mother often visited offices that eventually decided our fate several times a week.

After a while, our choices narrowed to Canada and the United States of America. Whichever country accepted our family first would be the place where we were going to put down our new roots. Back in Israel, my father finally took delivery of our furniture and possessions, sold everything we owned for any price he could get, and just barely scraped together enough money to buy a plane ticket to Athens.

When he finally arrived, he brought virtually nothing except for a prized family possession: our English-to-Russian dictionary. Since I was being home-schooled during our journeys, this book became an essential learning tool in my life. After my father joined us in Greece, he assigned me new words to memorize every day. He was confident that our move would come through, and that a brighter future awaited us.

Once our chance came, he was determined that a lack of language expertise was not going to hold me back.

Welcome to Canada!

After eight months of *Spanakopita* and paperwork, my family was accepted for immigration into Canada. We first arrived in Montréal, and were happy just to have a new land to call home. It was yet another edition of culture shock for my brother and me, suddenly immersed in a giant city full of people who spoke French, but we got by with the English we knew.

Our stay in Montréal was brief, however. Before long we were sent to Hull, Québec, as part of a government program that taught French to new arrivals and provided integration assistance. Hull was not so much a city itself as an amalgamation of several neighboring areas (and has since been renamed Gatineau). Just across the river from the Canadian capital of Ottawa, it was (and still is) a French-speaking community. In just a few days, all the hard work I had put into learning English seemed pointless.

We arrived in Canada with only $200 to our names and the clothes on our backs. My parents constantly struggled to make ends meet. Our home was located on the second floor of a house that had a separate entrance to the backyard. A long staircase took you to the entrance of our two-bedroom apartment, which we rented for $170 per month. What my mother and father earned barely covered that, along with the meals we ate at home.

It was not an easy time for my family. We had very little money, and often had to wear clothes that had been donated by others. One lasting memory that stays with me is of having socks and underwear that were full of holes and constantly needed mending. That is probably why I refuse to wear clothes with holes in them today. If one of my socks develops a tear, I throw them out and get a new pair. Strange as it sounds, it feels like a luxury every time, an extravagance I still cannot believe I am able to afford.

I have always found it fascinating the way little things stay with you like that. Because we lacked the funds to eat in restaurants, getting even the simplest takeout dinner seemed like a huge luxury. In fact, I remember one "gourmet meal" we had from Kentucky Fried Chicken. Many years later, after an out-of-town performance, I took my wife to KFC on Valentine's Day. It might not seem like the most romantic gesture to some, but it brought back a lot of memories and gave me a chance to share that part of my life with her.

To get to work, my father needed a car. So, our $200 savings were spent on an automobile that he and I fixed up together. It was old and rusty – with holes in the body that had been covered with chicken wire – but it had to do. I still remember that when we picked it up, it was parked against the wall. There were gears marked "P," "D," and "R," but we did not understand that these corresponded to *Park*, *Drive*, and *Reverse*. That was one translation the English-to-Russian dictionary did not provide.

Even though we did not have much, my parents always kept a positive attitude and we were very happy to have a new chance at life in Canada. Besides, as a child, I really did not have any other frame of perspective. I suppose I probably knew we were not rich, but I had not known anything different, and could not compare our situation to anyone else's.

Besides, I had other concerns. I was placed into the ninth grade, in a French-speaking school. It was difficult, but I knew I either had to succeed or die trying. I quickly picked up the French language, made friends, and even joined the chess club, winning a second-place trophy in a competition.

As great as it was to see a trophy with my name on it, I am most proud to say I made the honor roll that year. Despite my language deficiency, I was eager to learn, and wanted to catch up on all I had missed while we were traveling. Teachers noticed my academic and artistic inclinations and encouraged me constantly. One of my art teachers even provided me with some modeling clay. I brought it home and sculpted a realistic-looking hand that was displayed at the school fair that year. Unfortunately, one of the fingers broke off after just a couple of days, turning my classic creation into a piece of grunge art.

Arriving in Canada was a big adjustment, but it was one of the best things to ever happen to me. Not only did my family finally make it to a free country, but my meager beginnings have kept me humble and happy throughout my life. Although money still does not mean a lot to me, even to this day, I am able to appreciate the little windfalls and luxuries as they come. My happiness comes from my family, not material belongings, but I have a better perspective on both because of what my parents went through to put food on the table.

Fitting In

Integrating to life in the Western world was not easy, but I was blessed with an outgoing personality. At the same time that I was mastering a new language, I was learning how to fit into social groups, as well.

There were social interactions in and around school, of course, but I learned to especially love the time I spent on the bus. École Gamelin, my new French-speaking institution of learning in Québec, provided transport to and from my home every day. During these rides, I studied my classmates – especially the girls, with their sexy French accents and cryptic body language. Eventually, I figured out that a foreigner was somewhat exotic to them, as well. That gave me the confidence to return their flirting, even if it was in my own awkward way.

I found another outlet for social interaction when I was sent away for a few weeks in the summer to Camp B'nai Brith of Ottawa. They saved several spots each year for underprivileged kids, and I was granted one of them.

Away from my parents and teachers, I was free to interact with other kids in any way I pleased. Although there were counselors, they did not keep a particularly watchful eye. And so, we all learned to be independent, and a little bit mischievous.

If I had been worried about feeling like an outsider because of my status as an immigrant, or my lack of financial resources, those concerns were quickly melted away. The other kids did not seem to care a bit about where I had come from. Instead, they noticed that I bore an uncanny resemblance to Alfred E. Neuman, the fictitious Mad Magazine cover boy. For that reason, I became an instant celebrity around the camp. My new friends showed me the satirical magazine, introduced me to Archie comics, and even showed me other "reading material" they had brought to camp. At night, magazines like Playboy and Hustler were traded and exchanged to view by flashlight.

There were lots of other new experiences, too. Some of the campers had handheld video games. These were not nearly as advanced as the ones every teenager has on their phone today. For example, the football game had lines and dots that were moved with controllers on a handheld board. Still, I loved seeing the new technology and imagining what it might become.

For someone who had always loved music, hearing bands like The Eagles, The Beatles, and Led Zeppelin for the first time was nothing short of a revelation. I remember being extremely fond of the song *Rocky Raccoon*, belting it at the top of my lungs from my upper bunk.

That summer marked the first time in my life I could ever remember feeling like a "normal" teenager, and I still relish the carefree spirit that came with it. One of the things I had in common with my bunkmates was a love of pranks. We pulled them on each other constantly.

Once, when a friend and I returned from a full day of activities, we found our mattresses had been moved to the wooden beams below the roof of our cabin. On another occasion, we went to raid the girls' cabin in the middle of the night. Our "raid" was meant to include warming up toothpaste under our armpits and putting it on their sleeping faces.

We had learned from experience and rigorous testing that a sleeping person did not feel the warmed-up slime being applied. When we arrived, however, the girls were already awake, so we spent half the night talking to them instead.

The pranks went on and on. Boys slept and had their fingers dipped in warm water, or shaving cream applied to their hands while their noses were tickled with feathers. Every one of these surprises felt deliciously amusing to me, and I learned even more about the way people bond over laughter.

Summer camp was also my first real exposure to athletics, and especially water sports. Upon arriving, every new camper had to take a swimming test. I assured the lifeguards I did not need such an examination, proclaiming, "I swim like a fish!" I backed it up by passing my test with flying colors. The confidence it gave me was wonderful, and my bravado endeared me to our counselors from the first day.

I took to all the sports with great enthusiasm, but especially loved anything that let us get out onto the lake. I learned to sail that summer, and found it could be both calming and exhilarating, especially on a windy day. There was a distinct challenge in steadying the boat with my body weight while hanging on to nothing more than a rope, or zigzagging into the wind to achieve maximum speed. Sometimes, we tipped the sailboats over on purpose, only to bring them back upright in a grand revelation that felt like a magic trick. Doing so made me feel like the world's bravest sea captain every time.

I also discovered for the first time that it is absolutely thrilling to get up on a pair of skis while a boat pulls you and allows you to slice through parting waters. Being young and reckless, I liked to see how far I could push. It was particularly exciting to drop the ski and maneuver across the wakes on one leg, which I later learned is the art of slalom.

Some of the sports and activities allowed campers to compete against each other. One was a so-called "color war." In this game, the camp was divided into two different teams battling for supremacy. Kids wore different shirts with particular colors to identify them as being part of a faction. I was on the white team.

Our "war" was actually a combination of several different activities. We competed on land and water, trying to get an edge through races, baton relays, and even a "burn rope burn" contest, which involved building huge bonfires on the beach that eventually burned through thick twine strung up high in the air. We built teepees out of dry branches and lit them up, periodically adding wood kindling to get the flames burning higher and brighter while the rest of the camp cheered. At the end of these amazing days, counselors added up the points from different victories. Everyone was having fun, but we all definitely wanted to win.

One of the competitions within color war was American football, which I quickly learned was not all that similar to the sport that I thought was "football" and you probably refer to as soccer. I was not familiar with the rules of the game, and quizzed the team captain about what was required of me. One of my duties was to ruin a white shirt by putting a team insignia and player number on it so it could serve as my game jersey. This was an issue, given that I only had one white shirt, and it was normally reserved for Friday night dinners.

Finally, though, I relented, only to be faced with another dilemma: Each player had to pick a number. I had always been partial to the number 13. In fact, it was my *lucky* number, and I felt it had brought me good fortune through many stages and facets of my life. When I announced my choice, however, the other campers groaned. Thirteen, they assured me, was the *least* lucky number. Even though everyone seemed to object, I was adamant. They were so worried about our bad luck that a compromise had to be reached – the number on my shirt was going to be *13 ½*. Triumphant, I proudly drew it on both sides.

Going into the last day of our color war, my team was tied for first place after all of the athletic competitions and skill challenges. The final event was to be a play in the camp theater that had to be written and performed in a single day. Our score was the deciding factor that could push us over the top. I was selected to be the lead writer and producer.

I do not remember much about our production or its performance, except to say that it was about a very crazy person. The final scene involved me sitting alone in a straitjacket, presumably at an insane asylum. The "straitjacket" used for the show was actually a regular jacket I put on backward and tied behind me. I told myself jokes that I laughed at hysterically, delivering the same punchlines again and again, occasionally in different languages. My interpretation of an insane person must have been convincing, or at least amusing, because the entire theater roared with laughter. My team won the color war, with my performance tipping the scales in our favor.

Even with all the accolades and publicity I have received in the years since, I am still incredibly proud of that victory. That summer, I walked away with a great memento: a plaque with the inscription "most improved sailor" and title of "most likely to get his own TV show."

My natural gift for entertainment came out other times, too. Once, during a rainy day, I organized the kids around camp and convinced them to play a version of the local TV show *Mad Dash*. This was a contest where, instead of game pieces, the producers used people to move through a life-sized game board. I had a lot of fun with that, but also learned something from the experience: You can get people to coordinate and work together and in interesting ways if they are having fun.

All in all, that summer was a magical turning point in my life. I actually got to experience what it felt like to belong to a group in a way that I never had before. I was noticed for my personality, and made friends I have continued to stay in touch with over the years. After returning home, I was invited to lunches, parties, and sweet sixteen celebrations. In fact, I ran into one of my fellow campers not long ago. He simply remarked, "You've lost your accent, but otherwise you have not changed at all!"

Naturally, I was very much hoping to return to camp again the next year. When I found I could not afford it, or get in through another scholarship, I decided to take a different track: I went back to camp to work there. I applied for a job in the kitchen and was hired. So, while the other kids were playing tennis, swimming, and sailing, I was stacking dishes. It meant I could only use the facilities at pre-assigned hours, but I did not care. I was content. I still got to be a part of the experience, and was given my first taste of working for money.

Besides, the kitchen staff was a fun bunch. We listened to loud music into the late hours of the night, and amused ourselves by stacking milk crates as high as we could, or throwing water balloons at each other on hot days. On some cool evenings we built bonfires. There was also plenty of time to read books and feed my constant need for more information. At the end of the summer, I even brought back what felt like a small fortune – $500 – which I was able to use to buy a stereo.

Those were not the only musical benefits I received. As part of the camp experience, I connected with a visiting Jewish band, Shema Kolenu. They also performed under the name Uncle Moishy and his Mitzvah Men. The leader of the band, Moshe Tanenbaum, took a liking to me and invited me to play with them on several occasions (usually weddings or other social events). I filled in on flute when they did not have a clarinet and needed something close.

I also connected with a nice religious couple who wanted me to experience the Orthodox lifestyle and asked me to visit their home in Toronto. In Russia, religious expression had been prohibited. I was eager to find out what I had been missing, and thought it sounded like a great adventure.

I happily accepted their invitation, and took a bus to Toronto for the weekend that winter. Although our activities mainly centered on visiting historic landmarks and ice skating at the Nathan Phillips Square outdoor rink, they showed me a new city and gave me a peek into their kosher life. I found the first one easier to fall in love with than the second.

The young couple was extremely patient and understanding, explaining one kosher idea or practice after the next. For instance, I learned the time starting at sundown on Friday night and until sundown on Saturday is Shabbat, a day of rest. For 24 hours, electrical appliances were either not turned on or kept running continuously. Food was prepared in advance and kept warm all day. Lights in the kitchen and bathroom were always on. Elevators were set to be fully automatic, and all appliances were used on a continuous electrical current.

These practices were foreign to me, and sometimes difficult to adjust to. I remember one evening during my stay with them I used the bathroom to wash up before going to bed. The lights were on, of course, and I washed my hands and face before brushing my teeth. Upon exiting the bathroom, though, I absentmindedly turned the lights off. The couple kindly explained to me that they needed to remain on at all times during Shabbat because of their strict adherence to the day of rest. Even flipping the light switch was forbidden. I apologized profusely and without thinking turned the lights back on, to correct my earlier mistake.

Although I did not choose to pursue a kosher lifestyle, I was very glad for the experience. It taught me to love all religions and what they represent. They perpetuate traditions and keep families spending time together. They build a sense of community as people come together to bond over food and prayer.

Today, I consider myself spiritual rather than religious. But I embrace all religions and the comfort they provide. In fact, one of the first things that originally attracted me to my wife was that her family always had Friday night dinners together – a tradition that often grows in religious households. I know that beliefs can sometimes tear people apart, but they can also be a good starting point for bringing us all together.

Going Pro

Any experienced comedian or entertainer will tell you that finding your voice takes experience, perspective, and instincts. But sometimes, it also takes literal practice.

When I was 16, I came across an advertisement in the newspaper for the National Institute of Broadcasting. It simply said, "Develop your talents to get on radio and television." I called the number and the recording on the other end told me to "speak clearly after the tone, introduce yourself, and leave your contact details." I was convinced that someone would recognize my potential right away from the message and call me back, so I followed the instructions precisely.

I was mildly surprised when the return call actually *did* come and I was invited in for a formal audition. Upon arriving at the NIB offices, located in the heart of downtown Toronto, I saw numerous pictures of celebrity former students. Many, like Jim Carrey, had graduated and gone on to great stardom. I imagined my picture hanging on the wall as another proud alumnus. The tuition was $1,000, a huge sum at the time, but the school promised to help graduates get work after they had completed their studies. My only question was: Where can I sign up?

It all sounded incredibly glamorous and exciting to me. I do not know if my parents felt the same way, especially given the large sum of money that was required. My sneaking suspicion is they did not necessarily see a future for me in the broadcasting business, but thought the course might help me get rid of my accent.

So they helped pay the tuition, and I attended every class. When I was not learning at NIB, I was practicing at home constantly. I even configured a small microphone on my desk to simulate a radio station setup. The microphone was taped to a coat hanger, and plugged into the attached tape recorder that catalogued my future auditions and exams.

I absorbed the material and advice the instructors provided. Every weekend, I read practice news stories in the microphone, using scripts from actual on-air newscasts. They were full of tongue twisters, which helped me develop my speaking voice and diction. In class, we were shown camera angles and practiced with radio station microphones that felt authentic. Our instructors were experienced veterans who gave pointers. This was the training ground for my future media encounters, and gave me a set of audition tapes I could present to radio stations later.

Upon completion of the course, I sent out the best of my recordings to a few stations in the area and got several positive responses. Eventually, I was offered a job doing night shift broadcasting at a station in a small town in northern Ontario. However, I was still in high school and not yet ready to move out of my parents' house. The salary offered was barely enough to pay rent – in fact, it was so low that I needed to either steal or find another job just to eat. So I abandoned my dream of becoming a radio jockey, hoping I could come back to it at a later date.

It seemed I needed to find a different way to get my big break in entertainment. Luckily, I had something in mind...

Hypnotic Thoughts

I was always a voracious reader, and in high school I found a book in the library that piqued my interest: *The Search for Bridey Murphy* by Morey Bernstein. It was a true account of a hypnotist who performed a past-life regression with his female subject. That is, in the process of hypnosis, this woman was brought to a time before she was ever born.

Memory regression is a common therapeutic technique. In a state of hypnotic trance, the subject is guided to "turn back the clock" slowly, describing the environment and events around them. Through this process, they are transported to the time when they were a small child. They are quizzed about their surroundings, which helps tap into deep-rooted memories. Then, they are usually asked to describe an event that occurred around that time, such as a birthday party. They are also asked to relate who was present, and what feelings were associated with all that is happening.

In some cases, this process moves the mental imagery past the point when the subject was born. No one is really certain, at that moment, whether the resulting feelings and impressions come from the imagination working overtime or if they are reflections of a soul that is passed from one individual to another, holding on to previous persons and events over time.

In this book, the subject is regressed past the point of her birth and becomes another character altogether. This character calls herself Bridey Murphy and reveals the names of people in her life, along with locations and events of her past. The hypnotist, who is recording the sessions, follows up on the facts provided. They turn out to be true – everything she describes actually existed.

The book was published in 1956 and made quite a stir. In fact, it was adapted into a movie of the same name, and sparked many conversations about past lives and reincarnation. Later, I read a follow-up book by a skeptic and master debunker working under the name the Amazing Randi. His research showed the woman from the book had a nanny from the area she described while hypnotized. It is possible the nanny related the information to the child, who absorbed it subconsciously. Later, under hypnosis, she may have recollected this information and let her imagination fill in the blanks.

Since then, I have read and researched numerous books on the subject. Some seem to prove the possibility of past lives, while others rule it out.

Personally, I tend to think these accounts are the result of an overactive imagination. But I love that there are unknown possibilities, and think it is important for each person to form their own opinions and decisions.

Either way, I finished the book in one sitting. Being a skeptic, but also excited about the ideas and possibilities involved, I needed to find out more. I started devouring all I could on the subject of hypnosis. Finally, after a bit of study, I built up enough confidence to try hypnotizing someone myself.

My first subject was my brother, and the attempt was successful. It was the one and only time that I have ever involved a family member with my experiments. The whole thing was rather innocent, but it yielded some important lessons.

I had read in one of my books that if you can get someone to imagine they are holding a string attached to a large helium balloon, you can hypnotize them and watch their arm rise. I gave these suggestions to my brother, and then watched as his hand began lifting into the air, seemingly guided by its own power. At that point, I stopped immediately. Frankly, I got scared. Reading about hypnosis was one thing; realizing I was actually able to control someone's actions was quite another.

My further attempts at hypnosis continued at parties. I was hit or miss with my efforts to hypnotize others, but friends liked watching me practice. Sometimes, they even suggested new routines. Teens love to get together in groups to hang out and try things that are different or exciting. That is why they are great hypnotic subjects, and were the perfect training audience for me at the time.

One of the routines I developed during that time is still a staple in my show today: the "invisible man." I suggest to someone that I am invisible, but that they will be able to see whatever I touch. I then proceed to lift a pillow or cushion from the couch up into the air. To the hypnotized participant, it appears the pillow is floating in the air all by itself. If I touch them on the shoulder, they may ask the person next to them what they wanted. They *literally cannot see* that it is me poking them.

Hypnosis has a lot of interesting and therapeutic uses, but I found myself greatly enjoying the ability it brought to make people laugh. I had always loved learning about theater and improvisation, and those gave me the mindset I needed to visualize the outcome of a routine before I presented it. Knowing how to hypnotize made me popular and different in a good way. That got me invited to even more parties, which led to more practice and new routines.

Taking Center Stage

Eventually, I had enough hypnosis practice and comedic material to present a show. York University, which was fairly close to home, was having auditions for a talent show, so I signed up.

At the time, there was a very popular laundry detergent commercial on TV. During the ad, a pair of twins stood side by side in matching shirts that had been washed in different detergents. The two looked at each other and exclaimed: "I can't see the difference! Can you see the difference?"

I turned that well-known ad into the premise for my prize routine. Anytime I mentioned the laundry detergent's brand name, the hypnotized person (who was sitting down at the time) reacted to my cue. They jumped out of their chair, yelling "I can't see the difference! Can you see the difference?" Then, they would immediately apologize for their bizarre behavior.

During the audition, I successfully hypnotized a few volunteers and had the judges cracking up during my routine. I was invited to be part of the talent show, and could not wait to take the stage. I invited everyone I knew – including my parents, who had never seen me perform. I was proud of all that I had learned, and wanted *everybody* to see what I could do.

On the day of the show, I picked out my best clothes, prepared my materials, and even put together a quick "cheat sheet" to remind me of important details I needed to remember during my act. I arrived at the theater early, and could not believe how large it seemed. Every seat was filled. Looking into the crowd, I could see just about every person I knew in the house to catch my act.

I had been advised beforehand that I needed to come out partway through the show to pick a few volunteers from the audience. Then, I had to take them to a green room backstage, and have 10 or 20 minutes to hypnotize them. After that, I could do my skits in front of the theater audience with my participants already hypnotized (thus keeping the show moving along at a good pace).

Things did not go exactly as planned. I came out on stage between a couple of the other early acts, and asked for volunteers. However, to my dismay, only a few participants came forward. But I had just enough of them to go through my routines, and they were willing to be hypnotized, so I decided I was willing to work with them, too.

I took them on a long walk to the green room, sat them down, and started my hypnotic induction, which takes the first steps toward bringing a participant into a trance. However, just a minute or two in, a knock on the door startled everyone in the room. "They are announcing you already" was the message. I was nowhere near ready, as far as my participants were concerned, and the work I had already done putting them into hypnosis was largely negated by the sudden interruption.

In my head, I heard the words I have always believed and still live by today: "The show must go on!" I figured I could continue hypnotizing the group on stage, even though it would eat into the time I had planned for my comedic routines.

I entered the stage to thunderous applause. My family and friends were excited to see one of their own in the spotlight. I salvaged what I could with my hypnosis induction, and went straight into my prize routine – whenever I mentioned the name of the popular detergent, my volunteers were to jump out of their chairs and announce to the world that they did not see any difference at all.

Unfortunately, my volunteers were not hypnotized enough. They might not have been hypnotized *at all*. And so, they just sat there looking embarrassed for me that they did not feel compelled to do what I was commanding. The audience fell quiet, to the point where you could have heard a pin drop. The tension in the air was thick and stifling. I felt humiliated, shamed, and red-faced. *Everyone* I knew was in the audience that day, and I was getting no response from my hypnotic volunteers.

Suddenly, someone in the audience stood up. I could only see their silhouette through the bright lights shining in my eyes. In the silence of the hushed theater, he screamed out, "I can't see the difference! Can you see the difference?" The crowd went wild. More people stood up, screaming the same mocking phrase. My face went flush and my knees were buckling.

I felt as if I could break into tears, and the memory is still a painful one. But, one other thing I can recall vividly was that I *refused* to cancel my performance. I went through the rest of my routines and ended by saying I hoped the audience would see my show again in the future, but under better circumstances.

I walked off the stage humiliated, and determined to never go through that kind of experience again. I actually quit performing for half a year, which was crushing, given how excited I had been to finally show off my skills. I might not have ever performed again, had it not been for my friends and family. They encouraged me to keep trying. They reassured me that I had a special talent, and that it was a waste to give it up after one bad experience.

I did find the strength to take the stage again. However, I no longer invited people I knew to see my show for a long time afterward. Even when I found a full-time job, no one I worked with knew what I did in my spare time. Even though I learned later, through many years of show business, that good and bad performances are just part of the lifestyle, I was determined to never again be shamed in the same way in front of those who mean so much to me.

If You Do Not Succeed, Try and Try Again

My mother did not raise a quitter, and I loved the power of hypnosis to inspire joy and laughter in others too much to give it up. So, after my mental wounds healed and my confidence returned, I started entertaining at parties and get-togethers again.

At one of these gatherings, I met a young man whose father owned a small bar that was always looking for entertainers. Even though I was not old enough to drink at the establishment, they were willing to give me a chance to prove myself. It was not a big gig or a large paycheck – just $150 – but the fact that someone was willing to have me perform, promote the show, and even give me money felt like a major breakthrough.

For all of my excitement, though, I was also incredibly nervous. Not only had my first on-stage experience been a rough one, but I knew I did not have enough material to sustain a full night of performing. So, in order to be able to stretch my time, I visited a local magic shop and found some tricks I could insert into my routine. I faithfully practiced them until they came out naturally.

When the day came, I was actually relieved to get the chance to perform again. I successfully hypnotized the participants, and was able to elicit lots of deep belly laughs from the audience, even with my limited repertoire.

Halfway through my allotted time, I ran out of material and ended up repeating several routines more than once, which actually made them funnier. I learned by accident a trick many comedians, notably the wonderful David Letterman, developed over time. That is to repeat the punchline again and again, drawing the audience further along with each gag. Overall the show was a great success, but I vowed to write more material in the future so that I was never again going to find myself without something to say on stage.

Even though I aspired to be an entertainer in my heart, I knew it was not an easy way to make a living. My parents had firmly impressed upon me the need to have a profession to fall back on. So, as much as I loved the stage, I kept performing as a hobby while I moved on with my studies.

Back to School

Even though I had a lot of fun with hypnosis, and loved the idea of working in the media, I was not really aware that either one could be a realistic possibility for me. Once high school ended, I was somewhat at a loss as to what to do with my life. I knew I wanted to continue my education, and computers had always fascinated me. So I decided to make a career out of doing what I enjoyed. I needed to pay for college on my own, and could not afford an out-of-town university. But I determined that I could live at home and commute while going to school.

With that mindset, I sent out applications to local colleges offering computer programming degrees. I could get part-time jobs and get student loans to cover the rest. In 1983, I got accepted to Seneca College, and promptly enrolled in a Computer Programming and Analysis course.

I spent a lot of time on campus, and excelled at my studies. Most of my homework and research was conducted in the library and at the campus computer lab. I did not have much money, but had learned earlier in my life that it was more important to be enterprising. Instead of paying to go to evening events at the school, I became a writer for the campus newspaper. With those credentials, I was given free admission to all concerts and events. I just had to write a review that could be published afterward. Not only did this save me a lot of money, but it taught me a valuable lesson: Reviews generally had to be finished on the same night, so I learned to focus and handle the pressure of meeting tough print deadlines.

In addition to free passes to college events, the paper also got promotional records to review. That was a music lover's dream. Each month, new albums showed up at no cost to me. Over time, I accumulated a large collection of music on tape and record. I even made a bit of extra money by serving as a DJ at the campus pub.

Like most school papers, ours was minimally staffed. I received lots of additional duties. I helped with layouts, and even got promoted to copy editor. At the time, this seemed like a lot of work, but it was great training for my future. Part of promoting myself as a comedian involved writing my own press releases and skits to perform on stage. Learning to edit carefully made me a better wordsmith and artist. I learned that every word has a precise meaning, and that every phrase needs to be delivered carefully for maximum effect – on stage or off.

Even with all of these things going on, I still had to make ends meet. And so, I got a job cleaning a doughnut shop (creatively called "Mr. Doughnut") that was within walking distance of my home. It might not have been an executive position, but it seemed like a dream job at the time: I was paid in cash, and received as many free donuts and colas as I could handle.

The schedule was flexible. I could arrive anytime in the evening to do my duties, which involved taking out the garbage, mopping the floors, and sweeping the parking lot. Finishing these tasks normally took me about an hour, and I received five dollars for my troubles.

The owner of the shop, a kind Greek man, had given me the job without hesitation simply because I came in one afternoon asking for work. He valued my initiative. We grew to be friends, and he often invited me to come in and help out whenever he was shorthanded. This always happened in the middle of the night, when the donuts were being freshly made. Still hot and dipped in sugar, or covered with icing, we stacked them neatly in trays. During those times, we bonded over the few words of Greek I still knew and remembered.

Being around all of those sweets was a real thrill. But when I look back, what I really appreciate is a lesson I picked up and have learned time and time again: that the hardest-working people will respect you and help you if they see you are willing to match their effort. The real language barrier is not between those who speak English, Russian, or Greek – it is in those who are ambitious enough to work for what they want.

Going Pro

Even with my job and my studies to keep me busy, I was itching to perform again. I needed some new routines, and a place to perform them.

Developing new material for my act was a painstaking process. Early on, friends provided ideas, but now that I was on my own – even as a barely paid professional – I knew I needed to start crafting skits from the audience's point of view. So I started to write. In fact, I wrote *a lot*. I carried a pen and a stack of three-by-five-inch notecards with me everywhere I went. Whenever inspiration struck, I recorded my thoughts. Some were comedic gems, while others were not quite as powerful.

All the while, I kept scanning the newspapers for bars that could afford to advertise. I figured that if the establishment was making enough money to promote itself, they might hire an aspiring entertainer.

One of these venues was a bar called Woody's, located inside a Holiday Inn. The manager, who was also a disc jockey and in-house emcee by the name of Gary Gamble, was always looking for new ways to get patrons in the door early. He agreed to try my hypnosis show to see if it would be a draw. It was a regular monthly gig for which I received a meager sum of $200. I was ecstatic.

I was young and naïve. Being a regular attraction, I figured I could not let people see the same show twice. So I wrote a brand-new act for each and every performance. As word spread, Woody's became an incredibly popular destination on Sunday nights. The venue regularly reached capacity, and paying customers got turned away. I stayed on stage for anywhere between two to four hours, and gave the audience everything I had. Today, I believe you should always leave them wanting a little more. But back then, going through so much material was a great training exercise, and left me with a huge repertoire of comedic bits.

Remembering all of my routines was not easy. I used to put a table with glasses of water on the side of the stage. Next to them, I taped a set list for the show. Whenever I needed inspiration, or forgot where to go next, I walked over to my water, took a sip, and glanced at the set list. For a long time after, my contract rider specified a table with seven glasses of water. I am sure audience members wondered why I was so thirsty, but the reality was I needed those extra reminders to get through long performances.

After a while, I noticed that many people in the audience started requesting their favorite routines. And I got in the habit of asking patrons what they liked, or did not, in my performance. Through the process of paying attention to their requests, and hearing the brutally honest feedback that came from audience members who'd had a few drinks, I began to realize which bits were working and which ones were not.

Even though I have used hundreds of different routines over the years, I constantly keep experimenting, tweaking and perfecting my presentation. My performance tells a story that unfolds on so many different levels and transports the viewer into my world of make-believe and mind control. I do not want you to just watch a show, but to experience it. I want to imprint everyone in the audience with a positive message that they can take away as a "thank-you" for supporting my work.

Today, I am known as an author, comedian, hypnotist, and motivational speaker. I make my living by helping others get inspired, to smile, and be entertained. At times, I have performed upward of 300 shows per year, and traveled to venues around the world – from the Las Vegas Strip to corporate events halfway around the world.

All the things I love about my life and my career can be traced back to those long nights I spent on stage honing my craft. Some things worked and some things did not, but by starting at the bottom and being willing to test *everything*, I was able to make it to the top. I truly believe that it takes the same kind of determination and open-minded thinking to succeed in any other field. Work ethic, determination, and willingness to perfect your skills makes an ideal formula for success.

Becoming Incredible

Throughout my years at Seneca College, I kept performing. During the day, I studied computers and programming. But during the nights and weekends, the allure of performing was drawing me in with its gravity. I did not realize it at the time, of course, but I was eventually pulled into show business once and for all.

In the meantime, though, I needed to make a living. My course in computers offered an opportunity for a co-op position, which amounted to working as a paid intern for one semester and returning to school for the next. I jumped at the chance. Alternating between my studies and work duties meant skipping summer vacation, but that suited me just fine. I needed the cash more than I needed time off.

It was not just that I was paying for my own education, but that the small grant I had been given to pursue my degree was recalled due to a clerical error. Unlike a lot of the other students I knew, who regularly blew their grant money on parties and spring break vacations, I was actually using the funds I received to cover my tuition and to buy textbooks.

I applied for a number of different positions and was offered all of them. I attributed this success to my work ethic. Before any face-to-face meeting, I first researched the company and position extensively. That way, whenever any unexpected questions came along, I had a good context and background to fall back on.

Another trick I learned was to bring a slight attitude to every interview. I never wanted to come across as arrogant, but to let the faith I had in my own abilities come through. I truly believed I was the best person for every job, and that the companies needed me as much as I needed them. I exuded a confidence that said I was going to enhance the team by being part of it.

These habits made me popular with employers, but they also served me well throughout my comedy career. Preparedness and confidence are *everything* in show business, and they were qualities I developed out of necessity.

The internship I chose was with Hallmark Cards. My supervisor, Steve, brought me in to work with computers and immediately trusted me with a number of different tasks. I tried my best to excel at my duties, and to stand out. I was constantly worried they were not going to bring me back for another internship after my four months were completed – it was never a certainty – but he made sure I was always invited back.

Once I graduated, in the summer of 1986, Hallmark hired me straightaway at a competitive salary. However, the position would not be open until September. Because of the way my coursework had panned out, it meant I had a little over a month before starting my first full-time job. After alternating between studying and what amounted to a paid apprenticeship, along with my performances at night, I was glad to have a bit of time off.

Somehow, my parents scraped together a thousand dollars. They used it to buy me a ticket to California and offer me some spending money. It was a graduation gift that brought me lots of joy, and ended up making a big impression on my career.

I wanted to make the most of my budget, so instead of paying for hotels, I chose to stay with friends we had met long ago when we stayed in Greece while waiting for our immigration papers to come through. While my family ended up in Canada, they settled in San Diego, and we had stayed in touch over the years.

It was the trip of a lifetime for me. Even though I was fairly independent by that point, I can still remember my mother fussing over last-minute pointers of what to do and what to look out for. Along with my clothes and the little bit of spending money I had, I brought along my family's one expensive toy: a 35 mm camera I used to capture every memory I could.

California Dreaming

At that time, air travel was widely regarded as a luxury mode of transportation. I had been on planes before, but never as a tourist. I tried to soak in every bit of the experience I could – eating the food, viewing the movies displayed on small screens in the middle of the aisle, and watching North America roll by outside the windows. I even got a chance to meet the captain, who gladly took my picture in his seat, with all the buttons and electronic navigation instruments in the background. This was a long time before airline security got to be such a grave concern, and people were much more at ease about flying.

Once we landed, I found California to be just as magical as I had expected. The weather was hot, and tropical palm trees decorated the roadways. My trip to the state took me from San Diego all the way to San Francisco and back again. I saw the world-famous San Diego Zoo, Sea World, and gorgeous beaches. One day was spent crossing the border into Mexico to visit Tijuana, where I picked up a sombrero that still hangs on my office wall. Moving up the coast, I saw the Hearst Castle, Venice Beach, and finally my dream destination: Hollywood.

Like most tourists, I was eager to see the Walk of Fame. It was a chance for me to pay homage to some of my comedic heroes, many of whom I had grown up watching and used as my impromptu English tutors. To my delight, I also found that the area in front of Mann's Chinese Theatre, now Grauman's, was stocked with men and women holding clipboards, looking for people who were willing to be audience members for TV show tapings. They had lots of inside information about show business, and were happy to talk with me.

Being in Los Angeles did not just give me my first view of show business from the inside out; it also opened my eyes to what happens "off-camera" in big cities. One night, I was exhausted after a long day of sightseeing and in desperate need of a shower. Being on a limited budget, I found myself looking for cheap place to sleep. I came upon a small motel close to Grauman's Chinese Theatre. I was able to pay cash for the room. After washing up, I immediately fell asleep, only to be woken shortly after by non-stop noise going on outside. Being young and naïve as I was, I had not understood why the motel cost so little: Its *real* business was catering to ladies of the night. I learned an important life lesson that evening. Even though I still hate spending money needlessly, I am much more careful about which hotels I check in to.

Over the next few days, I took the opportunity to visit some of Southern California's famous comedy clubs. At the time, these seemed like hallowed halls for the biggest names in the business. Even though I have worked them all since then, I still feel a tiny shiver of delight watching the comedians dutifully writing out their sets before going on stage, or just hanging out at the bar. You never know who might drop in, or which agent will be in the building to say hello and scout new talent.

One evening, I dropped into the world-renowned Comedy Store, a club rich in show business history. The stage in that venue served as a springboard for Robin Williams, Jay Leno, David Letterman, and dozens of other working comics and actors. The format works like all the clubs in Los Angeles: The show starts in the evening and does not end until late in the morning hours. Comedians work the stage until a red light is turned on, signifying that it is time to wrap their act up.

On any given evening, you might see a gem of a performer, or a future headliner who is just making their start. The audience might be packed, or the room could be empty, depending on how well the show has been promoted and the number of tourists in town. Later, that room became like a church to me, a place where I witnessed one miracle after another. I spent many nights there watching comedians. I was never too shy to sit up front to get as close to the action as possible. Comedians often singled me out when doing crowd work when the audience was small. One night Judy Gold mocked my name, while the next I was the only white guy in the audience while Paul Mooney worked the stage.

On one of the evenings I spent at the Comedy Store during my California trip, I saw a relatively unknown performer drop in to do a set. His name was Sam Kinison, and he had just filmed a movie with Rodney Dangerfield called *Back to School*.

He began his performance by telling the crowd that other comedians simply wanted to make them laugh, but he wanted to make everyone sorry for witnessing his performance. He made it clear he was there to punish us. He did not just entertain; he destroyed the crowd with some of the edgiest material I have ever seen. He screamed at anyone who was not laughing with his trademark "Aaaaaaaw," seeming to feed off of the negative energy rather than scaling back his performance.

The bit that brought me to tears was his description of how to perform oral sex on a woman by using the alphabet with your tongue. I was not offended, but rather impressed with his ability to take material so taboo and craft it into a visual masterpiece that elicited uncontrollable laughter. He made a huge impression on me.

Later, I got a chance to hang out with the comics and speak to Sam personally. That was the one and only time I ever got to see him perform live, though I heard many stories about him in later years from my comic friends. Although our styles were very different, he did on stage what I always aspired to – he took a room full of strangers and got them to bond in laughter, often to the point of tears.

Years later, when I was performing in different comedy clubs myself, I often saw his name plastered on posters. He regularly appeared in the "upcoming events," arriving a week before or after I did. By then, he already had lots of money and fame. His appetite for partying was legendary –

drinking, drugs, strippers, rock stars, wrestlers, and even little people were all involved in his nightly blowouts.

Club owners told me he enjoyed himself so much that he regularly missed flights for his shows scheduled in Las Vegas. On those occasions, he chartered a plane with his Gold Visa card, at a cost of $50,000 for each trip. I wondered how that could be possible, until I heard he was making $250,000 for his Vegas appearance.

Sam died in April 1992 while heading to a gig when a drunk driver hit his car. Ironically enough, he had a popular bit about drunk driving that drove audiences wild.

Watching Johnny Carson at Work

One of my goals while in California was to see a taping of *The Tonight Show* with Johnny Carson. To get into the studio audience, you had to line up early in the day to get tickets. Taping started at 5 p.m., but the free tickets were handed out in the morning when the box office opened at 9. Even then, the studio gave out more tickets than there were seats available. That meant everyone was on standby, and admission was not guaranteed unless you waited in line from the moment you received your tickets until the doors opened.

I did not want to miss my opportunity, so I arrived at the NBC lot at 5 a.m. There were already a handful of people in line. Those ahead of me were just as excited as I was, discussing guests on the show and holding spots for one another when someone ran out to get coffee. Our shared love of the program, and determination to get in the audience, lent a certain sense of camaraderie to the occasion. When we finally got our standby tickets four hours later, we moved to a second line with another long wait ahead of us.

When the actual taping began, Ed McMahon came out to provide a greeting to the audience. Being only familiar with him as the show's sidekick, I was greatly surprised when I learned he was the warm-up act, as well. Not only did he give us all the information we needed to be a good studio audience and help with the taping, he provided a bit of comedy that got us laughing.

Eventually, the great man himself stepped out from behind the rainbow curtain. I was immediately impressed with Johnny Carson's ability to play to the camera and the audience at the same time. Later, when working on my own routines, I studied his mannerisms and delivery. I found he was able to deliver a joke and let the audience figure out their own punchline. In that way, one person could be laughing at something that was different from the man or woman sitting next to them. It was more genuine, because each punchline was based on your own life experience, rather than having an entertainer fill in the gaps for you.

Beyond that, Johnny's delivery could only be compared to a sprinkler. He scanned the audience from side to side, looking everyone in the eye and making each person feel as if he were talking directly to them. During commercials, he pulled a smokeless ashtray from inside his desk drawer, and sucked air from a constantly lit cigarette that was hidden just out of view. He simply opened the drawer, took a puff, and returned it to his desk while the audience was busy with another distraction.

I used to study Johnny's every movement and delivery, both in the studio that day and countless other nights after that watching television. He was a professional entertainer in every sense of the word, and able to make each performance a memorable one. His comedic timing was effortless, as were his delivery and execution. He created unparalleled laughs, and did it with class and style.

For a comedian or variety act who got the opportunity to appear on his show, it was like making it to the Super Bowl or the World Series. It was your big break into show business, and if you got the "okay" gesture from Johnny himself, it was the ultimate sign of approval. You were going places.

Johnny Carson died on January 23, 2005. The news of his passing quickly spread through the show business world. He had provided so much entertainment, with an amazing amount of longevity. He was an icon, stepping into people's bedrooms night after night and delivering laughs before they drifted off to sleep. I was one of many touched by his work. As an aspiring performer, I loved watching him work on television and while attending an occasional live taping. The example he set was one I have tried to live up to ever since.

 I would have loved to have gotten the chance to perform for his audience. Many years later, after Jay Leno took over *The Tonight Show*, I even attempted the unthinkable: Remembering how Johnny Carson had invited the Gypsy Kings onto his program after they entertained audience members who had been waiting in line outside the studio, I decided to hypnotize some of the men and women who were standing where I had stood so many years ago. My plan was to help pass the time, and to show off my talents and get a foot in the door.

Once inside the studio, Jay came out to greet the audience before taping began. I offered him my promo package, and pointed to some of the people whom I had hypnotized already. He took the materials, but declined to have me on the show. Later, when Jimmy Fallon became the host, I asked him about doing a segment during a chance meeting in California. He was receptive, but the producers have not invited me to perform on *The Tonight Show… yet.*

Moonlighting as the Incredible Boris

When I returned from California, it was time to start my new full-time job at Hallmark Cards. But, even though I was finally ready to begin my "serious" career, the thrill of show business was more deeply ingrained in me than ever before.

None of my coworkers actually knew I was an aspiring performer in my spare time. In fact, only a handful of people in my life were privy to this information. I tried to schedule comedy gigs for weekends, and when I could not I used one of my vacation days to make the performance work.

This might have been better for my job security, but it was also because I did not want a repeat of my horrific experience at that dreadful talent show years earlier. In any case, I did my job well and no one complained or asked questions.

Because Hallmark was a printing house, they had a program where employees were allowed to go into the company store during lunch and pick out greeting cards for personal use. I collected these for birthdays and other special occasions, but also used them as thank-you notes I could send to people that booked me for performances. Management also let you print a small batch of posters as an extra perk. I used mine to promote my career. The posters simply had my name, BORIS, in capital letters with a tag underneath that read "Mastermind of the Power of Suggestion."

The headshot I originally used to promote myself as a performer was a picture of me in a tuxedo. I looked extremely pale, and with a sad expression that did not really relate the comedic aspect of my show. I knew I needed a new photo, and promoters asked me for one constantly. Luckily, a friend of mine from work – a fellow programmer named Mark Yan – also dabbled in photography as a hobby. He had a keen eye, and was always up for something fun. The two of us clicked right away. He ended up taking my first professional headshot, snapping the photos in his garage on a cold morning. I still remember the way he used dry ice to make me look more mysterious while his mother fanned the vapors in my direction with the dustpan.

The photos were a big hit with booking agents, and Mark later turned his hobby into a profession. Today, he has a successful career taking pictures for a living. I sometimes wonder if he ever thinks back to our high-glamour photo shoot.

Even with his help, there was one piece of the puzzle that still had to fall into place. I needed a different moniker.

There is a lot that goes into a name. As a performer, your stage name is not just a pseudonym; it is your brand. It says something about you to the world. If you ever doubt this, give a listen to the Johnny Cash song

"A Boy Named Sue" that offers a humorous account of what your name can relate to other people.

I learned this lesson in an unusual way. While I was still in college, a friend and I started a small venture together. The idea was that we could meet with business owners and help them to analyze their systems and computers, looking for any inadequacies so they could make their operations run more smoothly. I was good with the technical side of things, and he had the gift of gab.

To make our generic company sound bigger than we actually were, we renamed ourselves. We printed up business cards that said "James Grant" and "Robert Clark." We did not get very far with our consulting work, but I found people responded to different names in much different ways. When they got a call from "Robert Clark the executive," there was a certain expectation that was more palpable than hearing from "Boris the college student."

That led me to try a little experiment. For a short time, I tried calling clubs and venues to get performance bookings by introducing myself as Robert Clark, my fictional representative. The phone call went something like this: "Hi, this is Robert Clark. I represent Boris the hypnotist, and would like to talk to you about having him perform on your stage…" I found it was easy to describe my talents in third person, rather than boasting about my own achievements or showmanship. It was all pretty innocent, and I dropped the act quickly as I found real agents who were willing to represent me.

It was a good lesson, though, because it gave me the nerve to call on some of the biggest people in show business and introduce myself. In fact, at one point I recall reaching out to David Copperfield, who is known as one of the world's greatest illusionists. I wanted to be his opening act.

Somehow, I managed to get through to the backstage telephone at the O'Keefe Centre in Toronto to relay my request. Mr. Copperfield was kind to me. He explained that people came to see his 90-minute performance, and as such he did not require an opening act because it would only take away from his time on stage. But he thanked me for my call, and wished me success before hanging up. It was one of the nicest rejections I have ever received in my career, and it served as a reminder that there is never harm in reaching for the sky… and that there is always time to be gracious to those who want to duplicate your success.

Still, I have always valued honesty, and show business runs on relationships. Being Robert Clark was never going to work for me.

I have always been proud of my name, Boris Cherniak. My last name is perfectly suited for the back of a hockey jersey. However, I noticed when I started performing that my last name was difficult for some to pronounce and spell. So for a while I joined the ranks of one-name performers I had seen have success, like Cher, Madonna, Sting, and Oprah. I started appearing under the simple name of "Boris," which at the time was filled with intrigue and mischief due to a popular segment on the Rocky and Bullwinkle cartoon. The show had a sinister character named Boris Badenov, who was always up to no good along with his sidekick, Natasha. Other famous men with the same name included Boris Yeltsin and the classic movie actor Boris Karloff. I thought it lent a sense of mystique and wonder to my persona before I ever appeared on stage.

The people who had to promote my shows – and make money selling tickets to them – thought differently. The single name "Boris" was too vague to describe what I did, and did not tell audiences why they should show up. So they often added a slew of colorful adjectives to describe my act: *Amazing* Boris, *Astounding* Boris, Boris *the Hypnotist*, and so on.

Finally, there got to be such a wide variety of names and ideas out there that I had to settle on one just for the sake of consistency and continuity of my brand. Another performer, Kreskin, already had "amazing" attached to his name. So, after careful consideration, I settled on the one adjective I thought sounded descriptive and intriguing. That is where the name "Incredible Boris" was born, and why you see my shows advertised that way on a marquee.

People still mix it up at times and use different versions. As long as they get the "Boris" part right, I am fine with it. In truth, they sometimes even misspell that, as well. To me, it is just a reminder that I need to keep working hard to make them remember exactly who I am… and that if I want to call myself "incredible," I had better work hard to live up to it every time I take the stage.

The Business of Show Business

After a while, I started outgrowing my day job *and* the local comedy gigs I was performing on nights, weekends, and "sick days." In order to accommodate a more flexible schedule, and take on some new work challenges, I eventually moved on from Hallmark and became an independent computer contractor and consultant.

At that time, it was a fairly unconventional move – most of the people I knew were "lifers" who planned on working at the same company until they retired. Instead, I went out looking for a number of different positions where I could utilize my unique skill set with technology while still booking shows on the side.

Most of my computer consulting contracts lasted between three and six months. Performing had started out as a hobby that was not meant to interfere with office work. But my two lives were starting to clash. Although I was able to book most of my shows during nights and weekends, and in nearby areas, going out on the road was starting to become a necessity. Even in a city as big as Toronto, there were only so many bookings to be had, and I could only appear at the same venue (and for the same audiences) so often. As a consequence, I began to branch out to other areas of eastern Canada, and even into the United States.

When that happened, I either had to take a sick day or figure out another way to miss being in the office. I often walked into interviews with new clients having several days already blacked out on my calendar. I told the people I met with that these were "previous engagements" when I was scheduled to be away. You might think that may have stopped me from being hired. However, no matter how many obstacles were in the way, clients were almost always willing to work with me. I had impeccable references, and drew on my work ethic to keep me ahead of the game.

I always delivered what I had been hired for, which gave me a reputation in the business world. No matter what industry you are working in, people make accommodations for your lifestyle if they recognize you have talent and can help them to get things done.

The upshot of spending so much time working and performing was that I had amassed a small fortune, or so I thought. It was enough to keep me afloat for a year, renting an apartment in downtown Toronto. So I decided to move out of my parents' house and start a life of my own. Not only did this give me a bit of independence, but living in a one-bedroom loft in the heart of the city put me within walking distance of a newly acquired job: a contract position with a government agency.

Those types of openings were prized, as they tended to be steady and frequently renewed. That meant a measure of stability for someone working on their own. I had the freedom to essentially manage myself, reporting only to high-level officials as needed. It should have been a dream opportunity for someone like me.

Unfortunately, I found I was miserable. The other men and women working in the department saw outside contractors as a threat to their own positions, and did what they could to make my job difficult. To get the simplest request fulfilled was like pulling teeth. And even worse, at the end of three months it was announced that there were cutbacks, and all contracted positions were going to be eliminated. Suddenly, I found myself completely and unexpectedly unemployed.

At the same time, it was getting harder and harder to separate my life as a computer programmer from my growing career as a performer. No matter how hard I tried to keep things under wraps, news of my "side activities" started to spread through my friends and co-workers. Luckily, they were extremely supportive. In fact, many of them showed up to see me perform several times.

Being on stage was all I thought of during the day, and it was taking up almost every free hour I could find when I was not at the office. At one point, I was booked to do a weekly show at a hotel on Toronto's airport strip. It was one of the hottest nightspots in the area at the time, with an elevated dance floor that also doubled as a stage. The whole place had the ambience of a fine Las Vegas showroom, with dim lighting on the perimeter, and velvet booths along the walls.

My comedy hypnosis show became the main attraction, and always packed the house to capacity. I used to open my shows with a magic trick, and always one that involved a volunteer from the audience. Some nights I used a mental prediction gag, while other times volunteers selected cards from a large deck. Occasionally, I walked around before shows to wow customers with mental magic and to bend spoons and keys. It was a nice distraction, and a way to fill time. As I mastered new routines and wrote more and more material, however, the magic tricks became less important. Misdirection was a fun way to entertain people by fooling them, but the hypnosis I was doing was *real*. Audiences had trouble telling the difference, so I dropped the magic bits altogether to make room for a more elaborate hypnotism presentation.

The audiences loved the extra material packed into each show, which now contained only comedy hypnosis. I learned a valuable lesson that in showmanship and life, once you master something, you do not need to dress it up with extra fluff. Let your talents and preparation speak for themselves.

It was around this time I got my first great piece of publicity. A reporter came to see my show, but was not able to make it inside – tickets were sold out! He was so impressed by this, and by the glowing feedback he heard from those who *had* seen me perform and returned to see me again, that he wrote a half-page article about my work. My show, which was already being filled to capacity, got even more popular.

On the one hand, I seemed to have a future in comedy. On the other, there seemed to be nothing but dead ends in my career with computers. A sudden dip in the state of the economy had made it impossible for me to get a new job, so I decided I was facing a classic "lemons and lemonade" type of situation. The number of positions available for computer work were limited and declining, so I "had" to go into show business full time.

It was a calculated risk, but making a living on the stage proved to be more difficult than I had expected. I was already performing on a regular basis, but getting new bookings was difficult. When times are tough, entertainment is the first item that gets eliminated, regardless of how thrilled people are to see you perform.

I struggled for a while until eventually running out of money. The "small fortune" I had saved turned out to have very real limitations, and I could not even meet the basic demands of rent and food. In that first year, I made $2,300 in comedy. It was not nearly enough to survive. But I was doing what I truly loved, which was making others laugh. So, after swallowing my pride and tucking my tail between my legs, I moved back in with my parents. I simply told them, "This is the only thing I ever want to do. Please believe in me."

To their credit, my parents *did* believe in me. They also suggested I might have to rethink my career choice at some later date. But they let me stick with it long enough to see my dream through. Today, my mother and father are still my biggest supporters, and I am thrilled when I see them in the audience. They gave me the desire, and the means, to go after what I really wanted in life. Seeing the look of pride on their faces, and the sense of accomplishment they get from my success, still pushes me forward to this day.

Nonetheless, regardless of what your parents, your family, or your loved ones think of you, you have to remember that *no one* will ever believe in your abilities as much as you do. If you are going to be a success in life, you have to have the confidence and drive to make it happen. You have to be the one to recognize that anything is possible. It might be that no one will believe in you, at first, and they certainly will not until you believe in yourself. Your dream has to be what pulls you out of bed in the morning, and keeps you working way into the night. All of your energy and passion has to be pointed in the right direction.

I have a naturally compulsive personality, which can be a kind of hidden gift. Many years ago, I saw a Garfield cartoon that read, "If it feels good, overdo it." That is essentially my motto for life and my approach to work. If you can hold on to that mindset, it will take you anywhere you want to go.

Where Does the Money Go?

When people outside of show business see your name on the marquee, or find out you are appearing on a television show, they naturally assume there is a lot of money involved. I suppose there is, in a way, but a lot of it does not end up in the performer's pocket. That is because there are managers, publicists, agents, travel coordinators, road managers, and webmasters who all take a cut… not to mention lawyers, accountants, assistants, and venue personnel.

Do not get me wrong: I am not asking you to feel sorry for those of us who make our living in the public eye, just to understand that being successful brings a lot of new challenges and considerations. The more you make, the more you have to share.

Many performers will utilize a manager, who is essentially a bridge between themselves and the world. They coordinate with agents, publicists, road managers, and others who are involved in the business end of show business. They might also give career advice, or make introductions.

Agents are more involved in booking performers directly. A performer can have many agents, since a lot of them will represent you on a non-exclusive basis. That just means that an agent has a relationship with a specific performer and will book them from time to time as needs arise. In other cases, a performer might have an exclusive agreement with a certain agent (or agency) that applies to a region or market.

For example, I have an exclusive agent who books me for colleges in the United States, but that person would not earn a commission on a comedy club date if I worked one. However, another agent might be responsible for comedy clubs, but not for corporate speeches, and so on. There are agents who specialize in theaters, fairs, casinos, and even cruise ships.

In a lot of ways, an agent can be a performer's best friend. Not only are they often able to negotiate better deals and terms than you could get on your own, but they can come up with bookings you might not find anywhere else. In fact, if you know a lot of agents and each one only brings you a few dates each year, you will still end up with a full calendar.

If agents work on singular bookings, then publicists try to get your name out into the world so club owners, not to mention the public at large, know and remember you exist. Their job is to book appearances for you on television shows, and to have articles and features written about you in magazines. The more press you get, the bigger and more prestigious your press kit becomes. And the better your press kit looks, the higher your fee for each appearance.

Of course, there are also club owners and managers. These are the men and women who bring acts into places with names like Laffs, Comedy Showcase, Banana's, Hyena's and Froggy Bottoms. They all have to make a profit to stay in business, of course, and most of them talk to each other frequently. Often, if you do well in one club, someone else will call because you have been recommended.

This is a simplified description of the various types of personalities you need to know and be friendly with to make it in show business. And it goes without saying that each of them has to receive a cut of the money you bring in. So, even a headliner, bringing in big dollars for each appearance, rarely earns as much as other people think it does.

I had to learn all of this quickly, along with the art of negotiation. When I finally moved into full-time comedy, my act was already solid. I was getting tons of stage time, and improving everything from the quality of my material to the way I delivered it. I had a slick promo package with a brochure, credits, articles, and positive show reviews. I even had a tape that showcased my act and included contact information. My fees started to increase, and my calendar filled up. The hard part was figuring out which dates I should accept, based on things like fees and offers.

Rather than talking up my own shows, I preferred to take a humble approach and let my credits speak for themselves. In many cases, my reputation preceded me, and I fielded calls from clients or agents who were willing to pay top dollar for my services. I delivered what I had promised – just as I had in my computer consulting work. As a result, I got invited back again and again, and one date turned into multiple bookings.

I have never done what I do for the money. I simply love to make people laugh, and when possible to motivate them and change their lives. I have bills to pay, of course, like every other adult, but I always try to put people first in my negotiations. When someone invites me to perform, what they are really buying is me. I want them to have the experience of dealing with a seasoned professional, and for the audience to get a first-rate show. Money is secondary to that, and in fact I've found that most clients are happy to pay a little extra for a smooth experience and an all-out effort.

Regardless of what business you are in, or what you are trying to achieve in your life, I hope you will adopt the same kind of attitude. When you prioritize relationships, and doing your best, over the short-term financial rewards, good things happen. It is possible that kind of thinking has cost me a little bit of money along the way. But in the game of life, it has made me so much richer.

Learning to Sell Yourself

One way for a performer to make a bit of extra money is through merchandise. If you give a good show, patrons often will want a memento of the performance. Many comics I knew sold T-shirts, bumper stickers, and recordings, often working their jokes and bits in so they seemed relevant. Unfortunately, this required them to "sell from the stage" and often sounding like an infomercial, which I did not want to do, since I felt it took away from the comedic value of my performance.

I wanted a tasteful product, and one that actually sold itself. After a bit of thought, I spent a small fortune developing and recording a self-hypnosis program that I am still proud of to this day. I wrote numerous scripts and did an unprecedented amount of research into the project, even turning my little apartment into a recording studio.

I bought the rights to a piece of music written specifically for the endeavor that served as my background track. I also bought microphones that were so sensitive I was not able to use them during the day – they picked up airplanes flying overhead and trucks idling on the street. I got so familiar with the equipment needed to produce the recording that I started to give each piece a different name. My favorite was the "voice improver," which was actually an equalizer that softened the sound of my words.

Even with my high-tech setup, I had to improvise using household items to produce the effects I wanted. One memory that still remains vividly in my mind is of trying everything I could think of to eliminate a popping sound when I spoke into the microphone. It seemed like nothing could solve the problem, until I finally wrapped a pair of clean underwear around the receiver and secured it with a rubber band. Problem solved!

The result is still one of the finest recordings I have ever produced to this day. It has evolved from tape to CD, and is now available as a download on my website in MP3 format, having been originally recorded digitally. Although I have recorded many other titles for the self-hypnosis series since then, the first remains one of my proudest achievements. All I wanted was to produce a high-quality product that helps those who listen to it, which it does. It might not be as good as a live hypnotherapy session by a trained specialist, but I am proud to say that it is an affordable and effective alternative.

It Is a Relationship Business

For all that I have learned about show business over the past few decades, what really jumps out to me is not the different contracts or events I negotiated. Instead, it is the people I have met and the experiences I have had along the way. It is cliché, but true: *Show* business is a *people* business. It is all about relationships. I suspect most other industries and careers are the same way.

Working as a performer is not much like having a "real job." Being a comedic hypnotist is in another category that is even farther off. On the one hand, other comedians sometimes look down on acts that do not revolve around standup comedy. Ventriloquists, jugglers, and hypnotists are all considered "prop acts" by other performers. The assumption is we will not be as funny because we need something besides our jokes to distract the audience.

I obviously disagree very much with that sentiment, and have found that if you are able to deliver great comedy, the barrier between yourself and other performers (not to mention club owners and industry professionals) starts to fade away. If you are funny, they give you some slack. And if you are kind, on top of being a skilled performer, friendships can be made. Entertainers will often spend hours, days, and even weeks traveling together, sharing condos, or working beside one another in the same bars and clubs. In the same way, it is normal to become friendly with club owners, agents, and bookers.

I have gone through several different managers in my career. I never did find one whose style and vision quite matched my own. But getting to know and work with them has been interesting. I can remember one of my managers who also doubled as a promoter. One Halloween, he arranged to have me brought into a large nightclub inside of a casket to advertise an upcoming show. I was wearing a straitjacket and "escaped" from my confines to the delight of thrilled patrons. When you are trying to get noticed, and convince people to pay for your brand of entertainment, you do anything you can to make an impression.

It was always difficult to find a publicist who could promote my hypnotism act. Again, it is just not a normal, run-of-the-mill type of show. Instead, it is a niche within comedy that requires a little bit of background and expertise.

On one of my trips through Los Angeles, however, a friend in the comedy business recommended I speak to a gentleman by the name of Ray Costa. He was a publicist that had a few up-and-coming clients, but his fees were still affordable and my friend thought we might hit it off. I was also intrigued with the idea of having a Los Angeles-based publicist. That meant something to the assignment editors who covered comedy acts around the country. They might take a call from Hollywood, even if they may have ignored someone down the street. We became fast friends and established a long-lasting personal and professional relationship. He even came to my wedding many years later.

Ray was one of the first to help me publicize my live appearances. Neither of us was a big name at the time, and probably neither of us was charging what we were worth. I supplied him with a list of upcoming appearances, and he and his team worked on getting press for me in the cities I was traveling to. This turned into appearances on radio and television shows, as well as printed magazine and newspaper articles. Once in a while, I even got mentioned on the evening news.

His work helped kick my career into another gear. Local readers and listeners came to my show, figuring it must have been great if they had heard about it on the news. Club owners, in turn, loved having people fill the seats, and that resulted in more return bookings. Sometimes, I worked a comedy club for a week, and then would be held over for another week "by popular demand." As my popularity grew, so did my fees. Although I was happy to make people laugh for any amount of money, I was finally starting to make a living. It was still tough to make ends meet while paying a publicist and factoring in things like travel costs and agent commissions, but I was getting there.

As for Ray, he went on to accomplish bigger things, too. In fact, I am sometimes amazed to recall our first meeting at a coffee shop on Sunset

Boulevard. Since then, he has worked at the Oscars, handled Grammy winners, and consulted with some of the biggest names in the business. Through it all, he has remained a great person and a fantastic friend. When I am in Los Angeles, I always drop in (usually unannounced) and steal him away for lunch whenever possible. Between the phone calls he fields from A-list celebrities, we catch up and remember the good old days when we were first getting started.

Places and Faces

I have gone through many different agents and managers throughout my career. In some cases, they had personalities that were as entertaining and comical as anything I delivered on my stage.

As I have mentioned, there are a lot of different agencies out there. And I have been lucky enough to work with so many of them at one time or another. Many handle specific markets, like comedy clubs, corporate events, state and county fairs, or colleges and universities – money attracts a crowd. Many agencies overlap in their spheres of influence. I developed a stellar reputation, always making sure the right agent got their referral or commission, while I delivered the client's vision on stage.

In a business where some people will climb over one another to make a few extra dollars, great relationships form for the long term because of trust. Trust in a performer's abilities on and off the stage leads to more work. This works in any business – integrity and talent open doors to a happy working relationship where people recommend your services confidently.

At times, the only way to keep things straight in my head, and on my calendar, was to keep detailed journals of who had called me and what we discussed. For instance, I had to differentiate between Jack Pasco at Entertainment Unlimited and Walter Pascoe from King Entertainment, who was entirely different from a third booker named King Broder. I might get a call from John Yoder at Funny Business in Michigan, or Anne May from a different Funny Business located in Canada. Some agents even had two first names, which could be challenging when I had calls to return to people like Ralph James and Roger Paul.

You sometimes hear horror stories about agents and other "showbiz types," but many of them were and are some of my favorite people in the world. For instance, Jack Pasco had hearing trouble. Even though he was getting old, he refused to wear hearing aids, even while speaking on the phone. A conversation with him always sounded like one coming through a scrambled phone line. I said one thing, and he heard something else. If I asked for clarification, I was apt to get a third, completely different response. This taught me to trust what was written in my contract, rather than what might be heard during our conversations. I can still remember pondering the terms faxed over in his agreements.

King Broder was a character all his own. He was exactly like the version of a Hollywood agent you probably have in your mind. He had reportedly managed Eddie Murphy several years before I had met him. Eventually, Eddie had dropped him as a representative, after which King had sued and reportedly won big – a fact he was always happy to remind you of. By the time I got to know him, he was simply doing bookings out of the goodness of his heart. He enjoyed meeting young comics, and I was one of his favorites. I always knew when King was on the other end of the line, because our conversation went something like this: "Babe, this is King Broder. I have got a fair in Long Island. Darling, you get to perform on a mobile stage for thousands of people. The money is quite good. Sweetheart, you get paid this much, but you have to find your own hotel." If I was not ready to accept immediately, for instance because I had to drive for 11 hours to make it from another show just to get there on time, he started to apply a bit of pressure. "Take the date, babe. Do it for me, darling," and so on.

On the other end of the spectrum, I once had a manager by the name of Kenny B who was a funeral director by day. He enjoyed show business, and managing talent was a way for him to get involved. Kenny liked my show, and promoted me to small theaters and nightclubs. He seemed to have connections everywhere and always had an entourage in tow. To publicize my appearances, I was put in the hands of a major Toronto publicist by the name of Gino Empry, an instantly likeable flamboyant personality with a malformed toupee.

Put together, we were an unconventional but effective team. Kenny persuaded someone to book me, and then Gino got busy dreaming up promotions. These included regular "publicity runs" where I shuffled between TV and radio stations in a limo owned by the funeral parlor. The two helped me to devise elaborate stunts, like the one that had me brought into a nightclub in a casket and a straitjacket to promote an upcoming Halloween show. It was a blast, and we all had a good time. Eventually, though, Kenny figured out he was not actually making very much from his side business and we all went our different ways.

The Other Side of Show Business

When you are up and coming in any business, and especially in entertainment, there are people out there who will take advantage. For all the wonderful relationships I have built through my career, I have to admit there were a few that can be chalked up to paying my dues.

Early on, I was often asked to perform in showcases. These are events agents put on to highlight a new talent or performer as a way of giving their act a "test drive." Sometimes they are paid, and sometimes they are not. Some showcase events might feature a single act, while others will have several entertainers showing off their skills one after the other.

I never minded taking part in these. In fact, I still occasionally perform showcase events today, although these are typically for big planning agencies that handle dozens or hundreds of corporate bookings. Back when I was new, though, I did showcases for college and universities, for agents who might be interested in representing me, and even for comedy club owners. As I mentioned, the fees were not usually large, but I wanted the exposure.

However, I quickly learned that things were not always what they seemed. For instance, I remember a college agent at one point asking me to do a showcase for free, and then finding out later he was paid a full fee for my show. On another occasion, an agent booked me for an event that only paid $300, or so he claimed. Later, I found out he had pocketed $900 for my appearance.

As frustrating as these interactions were, I never got angry. Instead, I chalked them up as learning experiences. Over time, I figured out you had to be careful about whom you trusted – just like the agents who had put their trust in me, they earned my trust in return as well. Unlike a lot of people who find success in show business, I did not have any childhood experience or family connections. So every expensive error I made was simply on-the-job training. It was a tough way to learn, but that is the way show business – and indeed, many parts of the real world – have to operate.

To me, the real lesson here is not that you shouldn't trust others. Instead, it is that you shouldn't trust people *unconditionally*. While there are always going to be those who will lie or take advantage, I do not have to be one of them, and neither do you. Businesses and relationships are what we make of them.

Who Is in Charge Here?

Through all of these bookings, contacts, and rehearsals, it was hard to find the right fit. But I finally found a reputable agency that was interested in putting me on their roster. They were a small boutique firm that specialized in the college market and dealt with only a small handful of artists. The woman who ran the agency had a husband who worked as a mentalist, and was also on her roster. I was thrilled to not only have a professional on my side, but also someone who had an understanding of my work. It seemed like the perfect match.

In a short period of time, my new agent booked me for a handful of dates. One of these was a show that was in New Paltz, New York, which was close to her office. Even though she had looked over my demo materials, she had never seen me perform in person. My show was the perfect opportunity for her and her husband to evaluate me up close and see what else they could do to get more bookings for me.

The show went off without a hitch. In fact, I was confident I had exceeded her expectations. But as it turned out, that might not have been a great thing.

At the time, my performance contained a long routine where I duplicated the Arsenio Hall talk show on stage. For younger readers, that was once an incredibly successful late-night television program. I hypnotized one participant to believe he was the host, Arsenio Hall, while the other hypnotized participants served as guests on the show. In my version of the program, these guests might be musical acts, comedians, or even sex therapists. It was an elaborate setup, which the audience loved. They even happily played the part of the "dog pound," who thrust their fists in the air between acts. As the announcer, I could direct the show and push it in the direction I needed.

During this part of the television program, however, I also regularly walked by the hypnotized participant who believed he was Arsenio Hall. Very discreetly, and *off microphone*, I suggested to him that I was interfering with the program and being disruptive. No one in the audience was aware of these suggestions. And so, they could not see the real reasons that my fake Arsenio Hall got more and more upset and agitated with me as his "show" went on, eventually screaming for security and getting me kicked off of "his" TV show. Eventually, he had me removed from the stage while the performance continued with me off stage in the back of the room. The audience roared with laughter – it was unlike anything they had seen before. This routine has progressed over the years to include hosts David Letterman and Jimmy Fallon and even morph into other shows like *American Idol,* where I played the part of Ryan Seacrest.

Following my performance in New Paltz, I called my agent to get her feedback. I expected a bit of gushing, or at the very least, some glowing compliments. Instead, what I received was the news that she would not be able to book me anymore, and was dropping me from her roster of performers. In her words, I had "lost control" on stage. I tried to explain that having the participants perform without the hypnotist on stage was the *exact point* of the bit, but she did not want to hear it.

At the time, I was disappointed to lose my relationship with the agency. After a few days of reflection, though, I chalked it up to the agent and her husband just sizing up the competition. And when they saw I could create the look and feel of chaos – while having my hypnotic subjects responding perfectly to my suggestions – it seemed so real and authentic that they either could not believe what they were seeing or were afraid of what it might mean for the business. Either way, I realized I had something special. They were not dropping me because I was not any good, but because my show was better than they had anticipated. I had a hook – I was able to make people believe that a hypnotist lost control.

From there, it only took me a while to find my first big agent, Ralph James. He was the mastermind behind the band Nickelback. Initially a bass player for a lesser-known group called Harlequin, he had given up a career on the road to work behind the scenes.

With his help, I was signed to a prominent company, appropriately called The Agency. It was headquartered in downtown Toronto, and booked acts for venues across the country. I regularly stopped by Ralph's office, trying to get a word in between the dozens and dozens of phone calls he fielded from other agents and club owners. Often, during these phone chats Ralph mentioned he had a great new comedy hypnotist he was representing, and that "the guy happens to be sitting in my office right now." He said they should book me, and they did.

Once on The Agency roster, I was booked along with major bands of the day, including Bryan Adams, Jeff Healey, April Wine, Barenaked Ladies, Tom Cochrane, Gowan, Colin James, Rush, Alannah Myles, Joan Jett & The Blackhearts, and many more. The only other variety acts in their roster were a child musical trio called Sharon, Lois and Bram, and the well-known sketch comedy group Kids in the Hall. Often, I was booked on off nights in venues where some of the greats had made their mark. I was not making a ton of money – in fact, finances were still tight – but my schedule was filling up and if I did well, the venues regularly had me return at a higher fee.

When I learned from that experience is that we are always rehearsing for someone. Everything you do in life is a showcase, regardless of what you are getting paid or who the audience is. If you want to be successful, and to stand out, you have to take your chances when you can. You will never be the Saturday night headliner if you can't prove yourself on a Wednesday night first.

Eventually, Ralph got too busy to represent me himself and passed me along to a newer agent who continued to book me. For a while, I crisscrossed the country and had lots of dates on my calendar, happily getting paid to do what I love most. Before long, though, The Agency split up and Ralph moved to Vancouver. Eventually, he came back to Toronto and formed his own company. I still consider him a great friend. His focus these days is on huge bands filling stadiums and arenas, while my act is more suitable for theaters, casinos, and corporate events.

Fun People in Funny Places

At the same time I was getting to know agents and managers, I was also making a lot of friends with comedy club owners and bookers. It was a fun business and a fun era, since clubs were experimenting with lots of different acts and formats.

Many names and memories still stand out. Randy Butler had a hot nightclub in Fort Worth with his brother that was called "604" because of its address on Main Street. They regularly ran comedy shows after which the staff cleared the tables to turn the space into a dance venue. His philosophy was: The people are already here, so why have them leave? It was better to continue the party and have a DJ play all night, and sell drinks to patrons, instead of having them take their business elsewhere.

The concept worked so well that he expanded to several locations across the Dallas area. I appeared there so often that The Fort Worth Star newspaper called me "the most-often returned performer" in the region.

Across the state, Bob and Sherri Warren ran an amazing club called Froggy Bottoms on the outskirts of Lubbock, Texas. Their business was close to Texas A&M University, and just outside of a dry county. That meant they could sell alcoholic drinks to thirsty patrons who could not buy them elsewhere. Sherri handled the business end of things, while Bob tackled emcee duties. He liked to joke that their daughter, Chivas, was named for the drink consumed before her conception. Even as a high school student, she was an ever-present figure at the club, and must have dozens of stories about celebrity comedians helping her with her homework over the years. It was a wonderful place where comics were always treated like family. I can remember once, during an off night, Bob and Sherri inviting me and another comic who served as the opening act to their house for Thanksgiving dinner. That was just the kind of people they were.

One of Bob's hosting duties included giving the odd housekeeping announcement and providing each act with a grand introduction to fire up the crowd. He took great pride in this job, but did not have the strongest memory. To ensure maximum accuracy and enthusiasm, he diligently wrote the name of each act on a piece of paper he carried with him on stage. Sometimes, however, these pieces of paper ended up being left on his office desk. On those occasions, he ran up to the microphone and mangled the name of the poor performer who was about to take the stage. Or, he simply looked to the side and asked them what their name was again.

One night, Bob got on stage to introduce me, but had forgotten the slip of paper and could not remember my name (to be fair, he saw many different performers every week). When he asked for a reminder from the stage, I refused to tell him. He asked again, but I still declined to give him my name. The audience, used to his big introductions and faulty memory, got a big chuckle out of our interaction. I thoroughly refused to be introduced, or to give my name at all. Finally, he had to let me take the stage as an unknown. We laughed about that for years to come.

I never liked to rent a car when I was on the road if I did not have to. But even traveling comics sometimes need to go to grocery stores, dry cleaners, and other normal, everyday places. So Bob often provided an old pickup truck for us to use while in town. The first time I ever needed it, he asked me, "Can you drive stick?" My default answer to any sort of question along those lines is always "Yes!" To be fair, I was familiar with the concept, if not the actual practice. And so, I learned to operate a manual transmission by stalling a few dozen times on the way to the mall in Lubbock.

On the next trip through town, I thought I should save myself some trouble and just rent a car. When I tried to, the woman behind the rental counter at the airport explained, in her thick Texas drawl, that all the cars on the lot had experienced "HELL damage" in a recent storm. When I saw the many different dents, I wondered for a moment what exactly they had done to make the gods so angry.

After one of my final appearances at Froggy Bottoms, I received an envelope with cash as payment for my performances. Having dealt with Bob and Sherri numerous times before, I simply placed it in my pocket without counting the money inside. Comics are normally paid after all customers have left, which might not be until 1 o'clock in the morning or even later, so there was not any reason to keep everyone up when I trusted them completely.

When I arrived back at my condo, however, I realized they had given me more than I was supposed to receive. I never wanted to be known as someone who was dishonest, or who took advantage. So, despite the late hour, I called Sherri at home. I apologized profusely for the time and the interruption, and then let her know I was calling because they had overpaid me. She simply told me, "That is your bonus. We did very well this week." For all the people you meet in life who want to take advantage, you never forget those who are ready to step in and show you a bit of kindness, too.

A club called Comedy Showcase in Houston, Texas, was another regular stop for me in the Lone Star State. I was usually there for two weeks at a time, twice a year. The owners were a couple named Danny and Blanca Martinez. Danny, a wonderful standup comic in his own right, was considered the godfather of Houston comedy. Their club might have had the most unique design I have ever seen. The inside was decorated like a cartoon town, which only added to the feeling of fun and levity. During the day, the club ran defensive driving classes that were taught by comedians to make a little bit of extra cash.

Comedy Showcase was a home and training ground to many of the funniest minds I ever met, and several I have been proud to call friends. Ralphie May, Jeff Burghart, Billy D. Washington, Martin Walsh, and Cajun Queen Caroline Picard were all local legends. One of my favorites was house emcee Dennis Fowler, who delivered jokes and one-liners in a rapid-fire format.

As the club's owner and manager, Danny liked to develop young talent. He showed new comics the ropes and let them mingle with seasoned pros who hung out in their small green room. He often told captivating stories of comedy legends that had passed through the club over the years. I can still remember him telling us about the time he had fired Bill Hicks one night, only to rehire him the next night. Bill had delivered comedy that was so dark, patrons left during his performance.

Bill Hicks was part of the legendary Texas Outlaws group of comics, the most famous of which was Sam Kinison, who had a colorful persona on and off stage. When another legendary Houston club, Comedy Workshop, suspended him for breaking a stool on stage and inciting a riot during one of his tirades, he tied himself to a cross across the street and doused himself with ketchup. Two weeks later he played the same club to a sold-out audience. The Outlaws were an incredibly funny bunch who also partied pretty hard. Many Outlaws worked at the Comedy Showcase when Comedy Workshop closed down. You often saw Ron Shock, Carl LaBove and Jimmy Pineapple on the schedule of upcoming events and whenever in town, they dropped in to do sets.

Cue Music

My shows are very musical. For that reason, I used to require a sound man – someone who was in the sound booth, paying attention to what I was doing at all times. Early in my career, when I arrived at a venue, I provided the soundman with a box of tapes and a cue sheet. During the performance, whenever I spoke a specific phrase, he played a track on cue (hence the name cue sheet).

Back in these early days, most clubs only had one tape deck. It was dedicated to playing music as patrons walked in. Between shows on multiple-show nights, I often went into the parking lot to rewind tapes in my rental car. Sometimes, when the car had no tape deck, I rewound them by hand – sticking a pencil in one side of the spool and twisting it like a noisemaker.

As my act grew and I developed more material, the job of the person in the sound booth got to be more and more complex. To help out, I made sure everything was clearly marked. This was partly because I wanted everything to go as smoothly as possible, and partly because many clubs did not have a dedicated sound engineer. Oftentimes, the club manager worked the booth, or delegated the task to someone who usually took tickets at the door.

Even with these precautions in place, employees working the sound booth were not familiar with my show and regularly missed cues. On one such occasion, I was performing at the officers club on the Canadian military base CFB Gagetown in Oromocto, New Brunswick. My act was running smoothly and everything was going according to plan. However, when it came to a crucial point in my performance that required a musical cue, the notes never came.

Because the sound booth was far away, in the back of the club, I could not tell whether the soundman was not there or simply failing to pay attention. When someone finally checked, it turned out he was lying on the floor – he had not been ignoring my show, he was paying *too much* attention and gotten hypnotized! When the audience found out, they went wild. I decided to "go with the flow" and use him as an integral part of my act while someone else took over in the sound booth to handle the rest of the cues for my show.

Although the event was fun and memorable, it made me realize I needed to put technology on my side. My working knowledge of computers turned out to be of great help – a radio frequency remote allows me today to trigger music at will without having to rely on others. If nothing else, though, the experience has taught me that even silence can be funny in the right setting.

On the Road and Over the Airwaves

I was fortunate to get into comedy at a point when the business was booming. Clubs were looking for people who could provide laughs to their paying guests. Often, instead of having to find something to do for a night, and pay for a hotel room on the road, working comedians took one-nighters to fill gaps in their schedules. Depending where you were, there were always agents and bookers willing to find little shows for you.

Many of these agents had close relationships with the clubs and venues in their own areas. Creative Entertainment worked in Florida and North Carolina. Tom Sobel's Comedy Caravan had Kentucky, while Keith Gisser booked events in Ohio. As a comedian, you called, faxed, or (later) emailed your availability to these professionals. If they had dates and availabilities that fit, you got offered work.

As you might already know and realize, there are large parts of North America without much in the way of comedy clubs. And so, you could find yourself traveling a great distance to make it to two different bookings that were within the same general region. For example, booker David Tribble had a series of one-night comedy performances in nightclubs and hotels throughout Northwest aptly nicknamed the "Tribble Run." Another agent named CW Kendall booked events in Texas, Oklahoma, and neighboring states. He might set me up for one show in Lubbock, Texas, and another the following day in Nacogdoches, TX, 500 miles away for a radio show in the morning. In the days before GPS, that eight hours of driving could be stressful – there was not any cushioning on the clock if you took a wrong turn or needed a nap.

On one of those trips, I arrived in Nacogdoches having gotten zero sleep. I showed up at a radio station ready to do four hours of on-air entertainment feeling giddy from exhaustion. Luckily, the host and I clicked, and were having more fun than should legally be allowed. His sidekick had just left the station that week, and I was offered a job as his replacement on the spot. It was actually something of a tough decision. Inside, I still harbored a dream of becoming a radio jockey, just like I had in my teenage years. And I thought it was a job I might really enjoy. However, I was finally becoming established in my performing career and thought I might even have a future in it. So, after considering the offer, I politely declined.

Even though I did not become a permanent on-air personality, I kept doing a lot of radio work. This was partly because the chances of getting on television were slim, but also because the radio was a great medium for promoting events. If you had something going on, radio stations were always looking for guests to drop by and announce it to the world.

My very first big radio appearance in Toronto was on the 680 CFTR AM morning drive show with Michael S. Cooper. He had the No. 1 program in the Toronto market at that point, a staple of which was the "5:10 Stupid Joke of the Day." I was a big fan and a regular listener. So, not knowing any better, I called the radio station and asked for a plug for an upcoming show I had at a club called Spectrum on Halloween. Being the gracious person he was, Michael did not just plug my show; he invited me to spend an hour with him on the air. It fit with the Halloween theme he had planned, and gave me a chance to promote my appearance while I was in the studio.

I do not actually remember what transpired on the air that day. I was inexperienced, and extremely nervous. However, it must not have gone too badly, because it helped to get the word out about my performance, which helped fill the club that weekend. At the end of my on-air debut, Michael told me that hundreds of thousands of listeners had just heard me. I lost my voice. That seemed unimaginable. I did not know it at the time, but I was not just getting a good bit of PR for the club where I was performing – I later met my wife at the same venue.

However, not every radio station appearance was hilarious or successful. As with any part of show business, there are obstacles that have to be handled, and things do not always go as smoothly as you would like.

After a few fun and entertaining stints on *The Morning Show with Dean Blundell* on 102.1 CFNY, producers kept asking for me to return. I did not have anything to promote, so I kept turning them down. However, they were very insistent, and eventually persuaded me to return when I had gotten back from a comedy tour. I dutifully wrote a few routines that could be performed on the air.

Just before the appearance, I was informed that a local celebrity who was also appearing on the show that morning had agreed to be hypnotized. It was 5 a.m. When the celebrity arrived, it turned out to be the son of Canada's Prime Minister, the then up-and-coming Ben Mulroney. He later became the host of television shows like *eTalk* and *Canadian Idol*, and was in the studio to plug his first TV show. I was jetlagged and not really at the top of my game. Even worse, Ben turned out to be less willing to be hypnotized than I had been led to believe. Needless to say, the routine I wrote did not get the kind of response I had hoped for. So, I spent the rest of the morning talking about the motivational aspects of hypnosis in an effort to salvage my appearance.

Another favorite was morning man Scruff Connors, who hosted a show on Q107, and later 97.7 HITZ FM, both in Ontario. He welcomed me to drop by anytime, so I often stopped in, usually on the way to perform in the United States.

Scruff liked to put on unconventional stunts to get ratings. For instance, he once did a big promotion announcing he was going to bring in the New Kids on the Block to the station, a boy band who were at the height of their stardom. Hundreds of fans gathered outside the station to get a glimpse of the group, only to see brand-new mothers with their newborn children delivered to the studio by limousine.

Radio is really theater of the mind. On his show, I made predictions and did mental magic tricks, like one where I sent an envelope predicting the day's headlines to the studio weeks in advance. We opened it live on the air to see whether I had been correct. Or I had the listening audience think of a number, and then reveal the number they were thinking of in real time on the air. "How did he do that?" Testimonials came over the telephone and patched right through. Using the law of averages, I could find the right digits about 70% of the time. It was all based on scientific principles, but the whole thing was great fun and good entertainment.

On one occasion, Scruff invited listeners to call in about something that was broken, saying that he was going to use my hypnotic powers to start them up. We expected to hear about lawnmowers and watches, but instead received a call from a woman complaining that her vibrator, which had brought her much joy in the past, had stopped working.

We used every innuendo allowed on the air, and possibly a few that were not. Scruff asked if she could insert it into the charger. I implored her to rub the prized possession lovingly. Then, I asked her to place it against the speaker of her radio so we could "zap it with our minds." Scruff added that he needed to be close to the phone's mouthpiece so we could hear the effects of our powers. Eventually, the studio speaker delivered a joyful purring noise accompanied by heavenly music added in by the producer to signify our "success."

Besides the great fun I had on the radio, I learned to expect the unexpected, and always be ready for anything. No matter how prepared you are, you may need to improvise to be successful. It is a great strategy to enjoy your life more due to the unpredictability of the moment as well as feeling spontaneous while confidently making decisions that impact the world around you.

Seizing Opportunity

There is an old joke that goes something like this: An old man lives in the village by the sea all his life. One day, rising waters flood the first level of his house. The old man is told by the authorities to leave and go to higher ground. Being devout and full of faith, he refuses. He says with great confidence that the creator will give him a sign when it is time to leave.

Still, the flooding does not cease. Before long, the water even starts to flood the second floor. As this is happening, a man in a boat comes by and offers to take him to safety. Still, the man declines. He once again expresses his firm belief that the creator will let him know when it is time to leave his home.

Finally, the man is forced to make his way to the roof as the water continues to rise. A helicopter comes to rescue him, but the old man tells them to move along. He is already safe, he assures them, because his creator will give him a sign if the flood gets dangerous.

Not long after, the man drowns. He finds himself standing in front of his God, who is ready to accept him into heaven. Before he enters, though, the old man is compelled to ask: "Why did you not give me a sign to escape the flood?"

To this, the creator replies: "I sent you plenty of signs. When the water flooded the first level, I sent a man to tell you to leave. When you moved up to the second floor, I sent another man in a boat. And when things were truly dire, I sent a helicopter but you refused it. I eventually figured you were too dumb to recognize the signs, so I decided it was time for you to join me here."

The moral of the story is that opportunities present themselves to us all the time. But they do not always look like sure things, or the way we expect them to. It is up to each of us to recognize them for what they are and act on them. Otherwise, they'll pass us by before we notice, and then our chances disappear.

The Road Less Travel-able

These days, I travel primarily by airplane, and then rent a vehicle or use a car service at my destination. However, that was not always an option earlier in my career. Budgets were smaller, and many of the events I was booked for were in small towns and remote places, rather than big cities, making it more efficient to simply drive. As a result, I have logged hundreds of thousands of miles on highways and interstates across North America.

At times, doing so much driving can be tedious. But long hours on the road also provide plenty of time to write new material, figure out ways to improve old routines, catch up on a to-do list, or just let your mind wander. And of course in the digital age, it is easier than ever to keep in touch with the rest of the world while on the road via smartphones.

In November 1990, I was continuing to gain momentum as a performer. Having earned the trust of agents, I was getting new dates all over the United States and Canada. I finally had enough material to headline shows on my own, and did not need supporting acts. Many of these bookings were in far-off places that did not get many bigger names. The budgets were not huge, but the events could be lots of fun. It was not unusual to see an entire community show up for a show, and to cheer and laugh enthusiastically. Performing in smaller venues is just how you pay your dues as an entertainer, and I was enjoying it.

During that time, I had a long string of dates booked that began in Toronto and ended in Ottawa. There happened to be a big storm brewing, and the skies provided an alternating mix of rain and snow. I found myself on Highway 401, en route to a gig at a high school.

I have always allowed plenty of time to get from one place to another whenever possible, so I don't have to endure the stress of showing up at the last minute. Even so, I found myself a little bit worried about the timing and the road conditions. At the time, I was driving a Chevy Astro van. It was perfect for my needs, given that I was always carrying maps, contracts, and promotional posters, not to mention my own personal sound system that I set up for every show.

The highway was busy with trucks and cars headed toward their destination. The weather was turning into something that could almost be called a blizzard, with a fine mist turning into slush on the road. My tires seemed to have a good enough grip, and I pushed along at the legal speed limit. Occasionally, a big rig came flying by, splashing my windshield with a dirty spray of sludge. Gradually, the traffic thinned out. With one of my favorite tunes flowing on the radio, I let myself settle into the drive.

Suddenly, my van hit a patch of black ice on the road. The back slid out sideways from behind me, until I was facing a perpendicular direction to the one I was traveling. The momentum continued to push the vehicle forward until it flipped. In that instant, a thought from my school days popped into my head: *An object in motion must stay in motion.*

Time slowed to a crawl in my mind. It felt as if I had several seconds to collect my thoughts and prepare for the inevitable crash. I was astute enough to guard my face from flying glass and debris by covering it with my hands. I pulled my legs out of the openings by the pedals so they were not crushed or mangled.

My van ended up flipping two and a half times, striking the ground on the passenger side and avoiding impact where I was sitting. My seatbelt tightened, but held me in place. However, I was flipping through the median and heading straight for oncoming traffic. To my great fortune, the van did not slide that far. By the time it had stopped spinning, I found myself hanging by my seatbelt, but seemingly intact. After a short struggle with the buckle, I freed myself and climbed out of my now windowless van, walking away from the vehicle to avoid any fire caused by leaking gas.

Looking back over the wreckage in a daze, I saw that my sound system, my briefcase, and all other personal effects and possessions were now scattered along the highway. Amazingly enough, though, I had escaped serious injury. There were a few bruises, but nothing more. Other drivers stopped in their cars to make sure I was alive and to offer their help. Before long, a policeman, an ambulance, and a tow truck arrived. I tried to assure everyone that I was all right, and that I needed to make it to my show, but the paramedics took me to the nearest hospital in Kingston, Ontario, insisting I was "in shock" and needed to be checked out. I did not fight them too much. In my mind, I figured I still had enough time to make my performance.

In those days, everything was done on paper. And as it happened, *my papers* were scattered all over the highway. I did not even have my agent's phone number to make a call and warn them of my predicament. So I mentally made plans about how I could find my way to the venue as the ambulance moved toward the hospital.

Once there, doctors verified that I was fit and functioning normally. I have always had a talent for thinking quickly on my feet, and called a car rental company that could deliver the vehicle directly to the medical care center. Given that I felt just fine, it seemed to take a very long time to get released by the doctors and have a car arrive. Still, I remembered the name of the school where I was set to perform, and called the telephone operator (remember, this was long before Google and Siri) to ask for the number. Unfortunately, there was no answer – I needed to head directly to the venue.

I set off from the hospital in my rental car, relying only on my memory of where I was supposed to go. I had managed to retrieve my briefcase and a carefully folded map from the mess on the highway, so I attempted to salvage what I could and use them as navigational aids.

Sadly, when I finally arrived I was a couple of hours late and the show had been canceled. I am sure the audience members must have been angry. My posters and advertisements had been ripped off the wall. In one place, half my face was still showing, but someone had scribbled an angry red "X" over it. I felt terrible. In the minds of the men and women who had paid to see me perform, the entertainer did not even have the decency to call ahead and let them know he was not going to make it.

Luckily, there was a janitor still present to clean up the room. He had met my agent, and knew how to get in touch with him. I called, and he told me to come to his house immediately. Devastated, I gave him a full disclosure of what had transpired, and ended up crashing on his couch.

When I woke up the next morning, I found I had not escaped the accident quite as unharmed as I had initially thought. I was in a lot of pain, limping and feeling like I had hundreds of bruises all over my body. Still, I wanted to make amends to the school, and to let them know how sorry I was for disappointing them. I drove over to see the principal without any appointment, staggering into his office like a student that needed to be reprimanded after a fight. I explained the circumstances that had led to me missing the show, and offered to make up the date anytime at my own expense. He was very sympathetic, but sadly the performance was never re-booked.

Lemons into Lemonade

To this day, turning up late for that performance remains one of my biggest disappointments. I have missed very few shows in my career, and hate that I was not able to make it up to the school. However, there was one positive that came from the incident. I had finished paying off my van three months before the accident. The insurance company considered it a complete write-off, and paid me $11,000. With that money, I bought a used car for $6,000, and spent the remaining money on promotional materials.

In the days before the Internet, putting together promotional packages was incredibly expensive. You had to have a video that depicted your accomplishments, a printed brochure, posters, photocopies of newspaper articles, and a cover letter to send to agents and brokers. These had to be diligently stuffed into bubble wrap envelopes and mailed to their destinations. The process of printing, designing, and editing videos alone could be lengthy and costly. All in all, it was a big investment.

Finding the money for all of these things could be difficult and even painful at times. But I knew I needed to invest in myself, and believed that I was going to make money from bookings that resulted in my marketing efforts. So, using the extra cash I had gotten from the insurance on my van, I prepared a large batch of promo packages and sent them to every comedy club and agent I could find.

I knew I could end up waiting months before knowing whether the strategy was effective. That is because agents and club owners had to find the time to look through the mailings, watch the videos, and then follow up with me... and that was only going to happen if they were interested enough to do so, and if I stood out among the dozens of *other* promotional packages they received every week.

However, within just a couple of weeks, a response came from a comedy club in Oklahoma City. The owner had some sort of a fallout with a comic and needed to find a headliner. I can't remember what the date or budget was, but I recall being tremendously excited when booking my last-minute flight. The show was at a club called Laffs, part of a chain that had other venues around the country.

Established comedy clubs regularly coordinate press for their headline acts. That week in Oklahoma City, my successful interviews on the radio generated a bit of excitement for my performance, to the point that the house was packed for the entire week. In fact, my show turned out to be such a draw that the club turned away about 300 people per show, even though I was performing several times a night over the weekend. Patrons bought tickets, drinks, and even my merchandise, which helped to supplement my income. After being paid at the end of the week, I was immediately re-booked, and for more money. The club's owner also recommended me to others that were part of the same group.

In an instant, my calendar was full. It was truly my "big break" moment, and I have been working steadily for decades since then.

In addition to seeing my income and profile increase, I was having a blast. Comedy clubs were great training ground to try new material. Back in those days, standup was a booming business and in order to satisfy demand, the clubs had a hefty performing schedule. It was not unusual for me to do two shows on Thursday, three per night on Friday and Saturday, and another two on Sunday. Audiences filled each performance, and whatever I learned in the first show I could apply in the second, and then perfect in the third. My act was getting better, audiences were having fun, and I was loving it.

My Better Half

Being a working performer put me in an interesting bind: Even though I was definitely and enthusiastically interested in the opposite sex, I was not really interested in having a girlfriend. It was not that I was against the idea of a relationship, exactly, just that it was not conducive with my lifestyle. I was always on the road, and that made it difficult to maintain relationships. My performing career always came first. In fact, I once broke up with someone I had been seeing on the spot when she asked when I was going to get a "real job."

It was not that I was having trouble meeting women. Once the show was finished, the customers left, and the doors closed, there was plenty of time to mingle. When you have a good night on the stage, women are drawn to you. So there were plenty of opportunities to spend time with young ladies who hung around to meet me, or who were just involved in the normal late hours partying that took place. The issue was that I wanted to find a partner, not just someone to spend a night with. My luck finally turned when I met my future wife, Daphna, at a party in

Toronto. I had just come back from a long tour, and a few friends and I decided to attend Law Bash, a gathering where legal students celebrated the end of the school year, held at a club called Spectrum where I performed regularly. We were not lawyers, or even students, but it seemed like a good place to hang out, have some fun, and maybe even meet girls. We were correct. As a matter fact, one of my friends *also* met a woman he ended up marrying that very night, as well.

In any case, I ended up dancing with a beautiful girl who had an amazing laugh. We hit it off right away, and exchanged phone numbers. The two of us had some friends in common, and quickly fell into the habit of talking regularly on the phone.

After a few such conversations, Daphna invited me to do a show at her house as part of her upcoming birthday party. I politely declined, informing her that I no longer performed at such small events. After thinking about it for a bit, she invited me to come to her birthday party anyway, and to bring my friends along. I was glad to see her again, and our attraction grew.

Even though I spent a lot of time on the road in those days, we saw each other often whenever I was back in Toronto. Somehow, she seemed to know when I was around and called me on the phone. Just when it seemed like every hour of my day was spent speaking to different agents and bookers, my phone rang one more time and her voice was on the other end. Keeping in touch with friends has never been my strongest suit, so I was glad that she seemed to keep tabs on me and take the initiative to reach out.

We dated on and off for a long time. It was difficult to build a relationship, given that I went away so often, but Daphna always seemed to be there when I came back. Our friends liked to joke that our time together was so much shorter than anyone else's that we had to count our relationship in dog years.

I did not take the relationship as seriously as she did for a while. She always made the effort to call first, reminding me that she cared. I eventually came to understand that she had grown up around performers, many of whom were friends of her family. She understood the show business life, and was willing to make accommodations.

What impressed me even more, though, was that she really did not care about who I was on stage. It was not my act or persona that attracted her to me. Instead, it was who I became off stage and behind the scenes that she wanted to get to know. That was essentially the opposite of the way most women felt about me.

Eventually, drawing on my own grand style and propensity for the dramatic, I proposed to her by way of a magic trick. I invited Daphna on stage at the end of one of my performances, told her what she meant to me, and produced a piece of paper that I had twisted into a rose. Then, I fell onto one knee and set the paper rose on fire, revealing the engagement ring beneath.

We were married on October 2, 1994. My publicist and old friend, Ray Costa, flew in for the occasion, as did some of my agents. Friends and family ate, danced, and celebrated with us. It was a wonderful day.

We were set to depart for a honeymoon to the Bahamas the next morning. It had to be a quick trip, as I had a tour already booked for the following week. Unfortunately, we overslept and missed our flight. I will never forget the moment my new bride opened her eyes, assessed the situation, and looked me straight in the eyes, saying, "I want a divorce." If I had not loved her before, her sense of humor in that moment won me over forever.

I booked the next available flight, and we made it to our destination… not to mention the start of a long and happy life together.

My First Big TV Break

Although I had done plenty of local segments on morning and afternoon shows across North America, appearing on *The Shirley Show* was my first mass-media exposure. You can obviously reach a lot more people through

TV than you can live, and achieving this milestone was a huge step in my career.

Shirley Solomon was an amazing interviewer who could have been described at one point as the "Oprah Winfrey of Canada." On her show, she touched on sensitive and current topics with the delicate attention they deserved. Her program had a warm feel to it, and remained on the air for many years. It was even syndicated by ABC in the United States. She had a lot of topical experts and celebrities as guests, and the subjects she tackled were groundbreaking for their time.

I ended up on her show after the producers contacted me, along with many other hypnotists. They wanted someone who could perform a hypnotic induction, live on television and without any preparation beforehand. To do something with so much uncertainty was rare and cutting edge at the time, so the producers wanted assurances that hypnosis could be successfully performed on real volunteers in the studio.

Apparently, I was the only one who was willing to accept. All the other hypnotists they had asked, who included some of the biggest names in the business and a few legends I admired, wanted the segment to be pre-taped. They were afraid of what might happen in real time.

I have always been one for a challenge, so I told them I could do it. I will admit, though, that after I hung up the phone I worried whether I could actually deliver on my promise. In the week ahead of the appearance, I went back and forth with representatives from the program and had discussions about how the show was going to proceed. In those days, it was not unusual for talk show producers to sabotage their guests in order to create controversy and drama. I was concerned that might happen in my case, or that something unexpected might take place with an audience member. Knowing that I had to be ready for anything, I ran through a million different situations in my mind until I felt I was fully prepared. Still, I was not quite sure what to expect.

On the day of the taping, I was kept separated from everyone else who was to appear on the program. While the other guests were on set and getting acquainted, I remained in the green room. If something was going to go wrong, it was going to happen in front of the cameras, rather than behind the scenes. Luckily, there were some great subjects in the audience and everything went smoothly. I drew on a few routines that were staples of my live show, and the resulting display of hypnosis was both powerful and wildly entertaining.

After that portion of the program had been filmed, I shared the on-stage panel with other experts and people providing testimonials. One was a man who had previously had his gallbladder removed without any anesthetic, using only the power of hypnosis to remove his pain. Another was a doctor who objected to public displays of hypnosis for entertainment.

Such sentiments were not unusual at the time. Hypnosis was not widely accepted within the medical community (and in some corners, still is not). There are also misconceptions about what it means to be hypnotized, primarily due to media portrayals of hypnotists such as Svengalis, controlling their helpless and unsuspecting victims. Luckily, there were several people in the audience who had actually seen me perform live. So when the doctor, unfamiliar with my show or etiquette, questioned my ability to treat subjects with dignity and respect, audience members stood up and defended me. One even turned the question around, asking him, "What stops a doctor from treating subjects unethically behind closed doors?"

Between the live demonstration and the audience members providing unprompted testimonials, the episode turned out to be a wonderful showcase for my abilities. In fact, after the program aired, my phone did not stop ringing. I got great video I could use to promote my act, and I received numerous offers to make appearances.

One such call even came from a filmmaker named Vladimir Kabelik. He was doing a documentary about hypnosis, and specifically how it might point to clues about past lives and reincarnation. He wanted a stage performer's perspective. Although I remain skeptical about that aspect of hypnosis, I had a wonderful time participating in the documentary, which was called *Coming Home*. It was a great way to get back to my roots and explore a topic that had fascinated me more than a decade before.

Learning About Comedy and Life

Life on the road hardens you, and gives you a unique point of view about other people's lives. Being a performer is not just a profession; it is a lifestyle. Clubs normally had two or three people performing in one night. Occasionally you might run into female performers, but in those days, the comics were mostly male. Although we sometimes stayed in motels, hotels, or apartments, bigger comedy clubs tended to have their own condos that housed performers who came in for extended periods of time (usually a week or longer). Outside of shows and performances, a weekly schedule included publicity and interviews. Even so, there was lots of time off for people to sleep, party, and mingle.

During this period, my average stay on the road was six to seven weeks. Following each tour, I returned home for a few days to do laundry, say hi to family and friends, and then head back on the road again. From time to time, I had work on cruise ships. While at sea, performers have lots of downtime without much to do. After several shows, people will start to recognize you and invite you to have dinner with them, or to give you feedback on your show.

Some entertainers have told me that standing in a line and shaking hands with audience members as they leave the showroom makes them feel like a flight attendant. But I have always enjoyed this part of the experience, and used it as a way to make myself sharper. In fact, even in comedy clubs, I enjoy the meet and greet time at the end of the night. The line of people who are headed out of the showroom are a wealth of information. They will happily provide accolades or insight about what they have just experienced.

Some of the ego-boosting compliments are great, but you can learn more by asking things like, "What moment did you find the most memorable?" Or, "What in my show struck you that it did not belong?" I have even asked people, "What do you think I could improve?"

As a comedian and writer, I have to listen to my audience's point of view if I am going to come up with material that strikes a chord and delivers an unforgettable experience. My stage routines have improved again and again because of the feedback others have given me. Some bits and routines have evolved, while others have been dropped altogether. That process keeps my show fresh in a way that was not possible otherwise. You only get so much time on stage. And in some cases, you only get one chance to entertain someone who has paid for the chance to laugh. I do not ever want those people to be disappointed. I strive to be the performer that lives in their hearts and minds long after the show is over.

There used to be another fascinating thing that happened after the audience left. As a comedian, I was usually paid at the end of the night, and in cash. There was often an interesting process that took place. The ritual began when the manager closed the door to his or her office. Then, the club's safe was opened. The first item to come out of the safe was a gun, and then the actual cash. Sometimes, a club owner might offer a little bag filled with drugs instead of cash, which I always refused. I have a compulsive personality, and never wanted to tempt fate by picking up a habit I could not control. However, I knew lots of comics who felt differently.

One truth I learned about the comedy world during that time was that the party continued long after the shows were finished. I never got into drugs or alcohol – my "high" was my exploding career, and I found myself pursuing bigger and better venues instead of momentary pleasures. A rule of thumb was that nothing got done before 10 in the morning, since most people worked late at night and then partied after that. But, when other comics were sleeping until the afternoon, I woke up early, wrote material, and contacted agents during the day.

Holding on to professional work habits helped me to find a competitive edge, especially when most of my colleagues were not doing the same. If you truly want to stand out in your business or field, look for ways to work harder and smarter than the competition. Do not follow the crowd; get ahead of them. That is the *real* key to seizing opportunities – seeing them where others do not.

Mind Games

One of the toughest things I have had to do in life was explain to my kids what Daddy does for a living. Officially, I am a comedian, a speaker, and a hypnotist. Really, though, I think of myself as someone who helps others. Comedy helps us all to approach life with a brighter outlook, while hypnosis (and the underlying understanding of psychology) lets me assist others in seeing the world in a new way and changing their behavior.

It took a while to explain to my daughters what I actually do. Eventually, through the process of asking questions, seeing my shows, and viewing videos online, they started to understand what my career is all about. In a way, I think that was the best training for the questions I occasionally get about hypnosis. It is an intangible subject, and kids do not give up on those easily. They'll ask question after question until they are satisfied with the answers you have provided. It does not matter whether *you* think you have explained something well enough; the conversation is not over until *they* understand.

I think people are curious about hypnosis because it seems so dramatic, especially when portrayed on television. In reality, however, hypnosis is a completely natural state. All of us do not just experience trance; we live in it, usually morphing from one trance state to another on a daily basis depending on the situations we are in. We create personas for ourselves, and then play the parts as if we were actors in a movie of life, the format of which can easily be altered depending on the scene or situation we are faced with at the moment.

Is Hypnosis Fake?

One of the things every hypnotist hears on a regular basis is: "It is probably fake." This is partly because it is difficult for audiences to truly believe and accept what they are seeing with their eyes when people are behaving in strange ways. Their minds look for an easy explanation. It also has to do with the fact that the public tends to associate hypnosis with the occult, rather than established science.

The fact of the matter is that hypnosis *is* real, and the subjects you see in my shows are simply acting in accordance with the messages I am giving to their subconscious minds for a short time. By confusing their conscious selves, I can allow them to accept other ideas and situations that they otherwise might not.

Once that occurs, I turn my show into something bordering on organized chaos. On television, you get a two-dimensional perspective, but in a live show I want the spectators to experience the complete sensory overload. I want the audience to have a hearty laugh, and to see what is possible when we let go of our everyday ideas and assumptions.

What you see on stage is the result of several different dynamics working together for humorous effect. Every show is different because I have to take what I have learned about hypnosis and balance it against the need to read my audience and participants. Each person will react differently to the same suggestions, which keeps things fresh and amusing.

Hypnosis itself is relatively easy to learn, although mastering it is a lengthy process. Over the course of decades, I have studied many different facets of psychology, body language, neuro-linguistic programming, and other disciplines. I am just bringing them together in a fun way. In other words, it is all science at work.

However, being a natural skeptic myself, I do not go out of my way to "prove" hypnosis to anyone. My job is to entertain, and to pique your curiosity, not to deliver lectures on brain waves. Some people will always believe hypnosis is not real. They think my volunteers have a repressed need for attention, or to act out their fantasies. I do not bother trying to convince them anymore. As long as they can enjoy the show, we both walk away happy.

Everyday Hypnosis

Because society dictates what is expected of us at any given time, we adapt our personalities to suit the situation at hand. In that way, we are influenced by patterns and expectations, to the point that we react to a reality that is constantly being created in our minds. Imagine for a moment that you are deeply engrossed in a great book where you can visualize all the characters and their interactions. Transfer that to your day-to-day life, and you have a good template for human behavior.

Understanding that, a hypnotist simply acts as a guide that helps an individual achieve an altered reality, or rearrange their current way of thinking. The hypnotist has simply figured out how to reach that state through suggestion – an order of verbiage and actions designed to achieve a specific effect. On stage during a comedic show, I simply create a different mindset for my volunteers that they react to. In a hypnotherapy setting, mental patterns are rearranged to alter subconscious thought processes and resulting actions.

To grasp exactly why this works, you have to realize there are two parts to the mind: the conscious and the subconscious. The conscious mind is what we are aware of, and the ongoing thought process that occurs in our brains. The subconscious mind, working behind the scenes, accepts everything blindly. It simply reacts. You could think of the conscious mind as a guard at the door of your reality, using reason to decide which suggestions and ideas make sense and which ones do not.

All a hypnotist is really doing is confusing the conscious mind so it cannot be sure where the suggestions are coming from. For instance, in a comedy show, I present participants with ridiculous ideas that do not make rational sense, like a person forgetting their own name or being unable to pronounce a certain word that is needed to win the grand prize in a contest. In those moments, I bypass their conscious thoughts. Their subconscious mind believes what I say, and they react accordingly.

You do not have to attend a comedic show to see a demonstration of hypnosis in action. In fact, hypnotic techniques are used widely in advertising. One of these is called anchoring, which is the repetition of a specific idea to get viewers to associate a mood with a product. For instance, a commercial that constantly hammers home the idea that drinking a certain beer is associated with showing up at parties next to handsome guys and sexy girls helps build that impression again and again. Repetition is very powerful when it comes to altering subconscious thoughts and feelings.

A hypnotist simply uses the same proven techniques to speed this process up. *Anyone* can learn to hypnotize. To the degree that I actually do anything "incredible," it is in having an ability to use simple hypnotic techniques in an exciting way for the audience's enjoyment. I use improvisational skills, read body language, and act on visual cues to keep the show moving in a fun way. My real superpower is a sense of humor, not any form of mind control.

A Student of Human Behavior

I love watching people. I always have. I especially like experiencing, and viewing, the sense of culture shock that occurs when people are taken out of their normal environment. You can pick up a lot as an outsider that you might not notice in everyday surroundings. And, by just studying the way people behave, you can home in on little cues that might not have seemed obvious.

For this reason, I really enjoy studying strangers at airports and other public places. I especially like watching body language, which can give you insights into the connection between thoughts and actions. If you pay attention to the way people move and express themselves long enough, the ability becomes innate. Then, you can tell a lot about individuals and their moods simply by watching their hands, shoulders, and facial tics. As a performer, you can even use this knowledge to achieve specific outcomes when needed.

As a result of working on stage for so many years, I choose my words carefully. I always try to be vigilant about what is coming out of my mouth, so I can become a minimalist with my speech and relate exactly what I mean. For example, to deliver a command to hypnotized volunteers, I have to state it in a way that they can understand, relate to, and be able to comply with. The suggestion has to be interpreted universally, and taken literally.

Once, while performing in St. Lucia in the Caribbean, I successfully hypnotized a volunteer who did not speak any English. I realized this only after I gave him a funny routine to perform to which he did not comply – he did not understand the meaning of my command! When I brought in a translator to help with the performance, he proved to be a fantastic subject.

You can follow my example. Even if you are not hypnotizing others, you can change the words you use to make your life a better one. You can use language to achieve a positive attitude, and to instill it in you and the people around you. Whenever I arrive to a new venue or event, people naturally ask: "How are you doing?" My response is always: "Excellent!" This is a powerful habit. For one thing, when you repeat something often enough, you start to believe it. And your positive attitude spreads to others around you.

There is an entire science based on language use and hypnotic patterns. It is called neuro-linguistic programming, or NLP, and is devoted to achieving a specific action by using words with precise meanings. You can take language to paint an unmistakable picture in a person's mind, and then have them react in a specific and predictable way. Often, these reactions will overcome natural intuition. As you might guess, advertisers and sales professionals use these powers to great effect. For instance, a car salesman will often call you by your first name repeatedly to give a feeling of intimacy and personalization.

That is just one example, but it works in a lot of different ways and settings. By being observant, and learning how to transmit and receive subtle signals, we become more effective and persuasive people. Our stance and demeanor reflect our thoughts, which we present to the world unconsciously. By deciphering responses and being observant, a person's expressions and body language will tell a story that comes together like a jigsaw puzzle.

Although hypnosis, body language, and NLP are all rooted in science, an understanding of their different elements is beginning to make its way into popular culture. When you see television shows like *The Mentalist* and *Lie to Me*, you will observe that the main character translates reactions to help solve difficult cases. They can tell when people are being deceptive by the position of their eyes, which indicate access to a specific part of the brain. In other words, they use their training to spot when criminals are unconsciously using eye muscles to relate their *real* thoughts and intentions.

While you certainly cannot believe everything you see on television, these ideas are rooted in proven principles. Body posture and subconscious actions relate unconscious or hidden feelings. And being familiar with the use of words can indeed help you to program another person's thinking for your benefit.

My work relies on a lot of mind games, word play, and improvisational comedy. However, the underlying hypnosis and mental phenomena are quite real. In fact, if you can learn about how it works behind the scenes, even in a simple way, you can apply the principles to greatly boost your career and personal relationships.

You Are Richer Than You Think

Many years ago, Scotiabank in Canada put together a brilliant marketing campaign. They ran ads that simply proclaimed, "You are richer than you think."

At the time, that felt like some kind of sarcastic taunt. I had never felt more broke. It was during a period when things were tough, and I had maxed out my credit line. I was getting bookings, but my cash flow was uneven. My only option, it seemed, was to create a bit of artificial short-term income by selling my house, moving into a smaller place, and using some of the equity I had built up to pay bills.

Just as I was working on the paperwork, and feeling pessimistic about my finances, a friend happened to ask why I did not just speak with my bank to renegotiate the terms of my credit line by using the equity in my house as collateral. I might be able to lower my payments, they suggested. I did not think there was much chance of that happening, but what did I have to lose?

It only took a relatively short conversation, and a few forms, to successfully change the terms of my credit line, secured by my home. Suddenly, I was able to remain in my same house, but meet my obligations comfortably and ease the pressure of bills while my income caught up. With that room to breathe, it did not take long for my finances to start moving in the right direction.

The important part of this story is that, at least in the short term, my financial status did not change. What *did* shift was my thinking and perspective on the situation. Instead of focusing on what was going wrong, or the negative outcomes I was convinced were destined to take place, I turned my attention to possible solutions. Once that happened, things began to fall in line and move in the right direction.

You undoubtedly have challenges you are dealing with right now, or will in the future. Never forget that the way you feel about them is every bit as important as the obstacles themselves. Once you can concentrate on the positive aspects of what is right in front of you, you just might find that you really *are* richer than you think.

Prophetic Thinking (AKA, How to Talk to Yourself)

Each of us has an ongoing dialogue in our own minds. That is, we talk to ourselves all the time, even if it is not out loud. This is completely normal, but can have big (and usually unseen) effects on our lives.

Here's why: In between the random thoughts and considerations we make, the "what ifs" and insults at other drivers on the road or shoppers in the grocery line, we often use our self-talk to give voice to doubt and insecurity. We bring ourselves down from the inside out. The more negative these emotions are, the more we believe them and the less adequate and fulfilled we feel.

With that in mind, it is important to choose the words you give yourself wisely. No one is listening in but you, so why reinforce past mistakes when you could encourage positive thoughts and actions?

Whether we are aware of it or not, we pay a lot of attention to the messages we transmit to our own minds. You can actually train your brain, through repetition, to latch on to better ideas and more positive notions. You can build up your own self-esteem, improve your confidence, and tell yourself that you complete tasks well and remain in control of every situation.

We are all prophets, with a gift of seeing the future and speaking it out loud. The trick is to reinforce an idea again and again, in your own mind, until it becomes reality. The more you think about something, the more determined you are to achieve it. Once you fix it firmly in your mind, at an emotional level, your subconscious will take over. Your "prophecy" will come true, because it has already been made real through visualization.

Choose your goals carefully, and then reinforce them until your brain has no choice but to push you in the right direction.

Stay Positive and Keep Laughing

Positivity is contagious. It does not just spread from one person to another, but from one moment to the next. When you are in a good mood, you are likely to *stay* in a good mood. And of course, the opposite can also be true.

That is one of the reasons I always encourage everyone to make time for laughter. It is great for your state of mind and creativity, while also boosting your energy levels and immune system. Best of all, laughing costs nothing. You can do it anywhere, and you will often find that others will join in when you do. As a comedy hypnotist *and* a regular observer of people, I can tell you definitively that humans are naturally funny. If you just give yourself the chance to find the humor in life, you certainly will.

Probably my favorite thing about laughter is that it helps us to express joy. And what is life, really, without a bit of joy? It is easy to get so absorbed in everyday tasks that we forget to enjoy the moment we are in. That is especially true as we get older, or fall into routines. We can become immune to the things that we really love and draw enjoyment from if they become part of our day-to-day reality.

I make it a point to try to have fun with everything I do. If I can't, then it is a sign that it is time for me to make a change and move on to something else. Even one of my biggest dreams, to own my own comedy club, eventually grew stale. Look for anything that has gone stagnant in your own life and see if you can do something differently. It can be hard to change, but it is well worth it if you can find a new spark or inspiration.

Dealing with Others

No matter how positive you are, and how much fun you are having, it is difficult to find success in life without the cooperation of others. And so, it's important to know how to treat the people in your life. Obviously, I could write a whole other book on the subject (as many people have). However, there are a few things I have noticed in my time on the planet that seem to be universal, and might be able to point you in the right direction.

The first is that it is important to spend time not just with people you like, but who also mirror your values. If you want to become hard-working and successful, hang out with others who have the same qualities. We tend to rub off on one another more than most people realize, and choosing the right "inner circle" is an important part of becoming successful.

I can also tell you that honesty is an underrated quality. We all tell white lies. Sometimes, we tell them to cover up our inadequacies. Other times, it is because we want to make others feel good about us, or themselves, or to avoid hurting someone's feelings. Occasionally, we might embellish or exaggerate to get a point across.

While some white lies are probably unavoidable, being an honest person liberates you and sets you apart from the crowd. I am not going to tell you that brutal honesty will *always* make things easier – it may even hold you back now and again – but in the long run, it is the best policy. If others get the sense that you are constantly sugarcoating things, they will subconsciously sense something is not right and avoid trusting you. On the other hand, if the people in your life know that you are going to tell them the truth, they'll always respect you even if they do not agree with you.

Never give up your personal integrity. This relates to your honesty, of course, but also your actions. I firmly believe one of the reasons I have been able to remain successful in a tough business for so long is that I absolutely refused to lie, cheat, or steal to get ahead. I never disrespected anyone who had a lesser job or position, and I did not begrudge others for triumphing where I could not. Even when I was disappointed, I did not let it stop me from being gracious. People remember that kind of thing, and it always comes back to you in a big way.

And finally, when working with others, remember that "maybe" often means "yes." I got this concept from my wife when we were dating, when she used to say it to me as a joke. Before you get too upset, recognize that I am not telling you to violate someone else's personal space, or saying that

I stalked her until she agreed to go out with me. What I *am* saying is that you should never give up on any idea too quickly or easily.

Until someone tells me "no," I always hold out for the possibility of a positive outcome. By holding on to that attitude, and being persistent, I have been able to make my way into comedy clubs, onto TV, and even into my wife's heart.

When someone is not receptive to your ideas, or really does not want to work with you, they will tell you "no." It can be hard to hear, but pushing for a negative response brings clarity to the situation and shows confidence in your abilities. Plus, by asking for a definitive answer, you may find out that maybe really does mean yes... even if that yes is coming at a later date.

Daring to Do the Impossible

As I have already said, knowing about the science behind hypnosis is one thing, but using it to a creative and comedic effect is quite another. Sometimes my best material seems to almost write itself – the inspiration comes to me and the bit has been conceived in just a few minutes.

One of my favorite routines, and one I use as a signature bit, actually came from a dare. I was performing at ACME Comedy Company in downtown Minneapolis, where I had been booked for two solid weeks, when I developed this routine. The club is a great, intimate venue. The audience is squeezed tightly together, which helps laughter to spread like wildfire. Plus, the bar and dining room are separated from the showroom, so the audience's attention is never disturbed by noises coming from bartenders or other staff.

During my two-week stay, comics were being housed in a private condo close by. I regularly walked over to the club during the day to have lunch and coffee, getting to know the other comics and staff while hanging out and making new friends. That kind of human interaction can be a great relief from boredom when you spend long hours working on material or doing publicity runs. In fact, I have often found that comics will hang out with each other before and after shows, just discussing the business or specific routines that were performed on stage. It is always a great way to catch up and find out who is doing what.

During that week, I became friendly with a comedian named Tim Mitchell. He and I spent many hours discussing the state of the industry. Tim also doubled as a soundman, and had witnessed countless shows at the club. He related to me that he and a number of other Minneapolis comedians had finally stumbled onto the one subject that could not be made funny. He rattled off the names of many top performers, including Lewis Black, Nick Swardson, Louis CK, and Doug Stanhope, who had tried to make audiences snicker at the subject, only to get the equivalent of chirping crickets.

This daunting comedic roadblock was none other than the subject of white-water rafting. It was deemed completely un-funny, the opposite of comedy gold.

I just could not accept the thought. With the challenge set in my mind, I began scribbling different ideas on a cocktail napkin. What I eventually devised became a staple of my show to this very day, and the first performance was actually worked from a napkin I scribbled my ideas on earlier.

As any seasoned performer can tell you, the best way to try a new routine on stage is to sandwich it between two other bits that are proven and sure to bring laughs. So, that is exactly what I did. I regularly perform a hot and cold routine, where my hypnotized volunteers envision themselves on a beach. They sweat and apply imaginary suntan lotion on themselves and each other while sipping nonexistent umbrella drinks. Suddenly, they are magically transported to arctic Alaska, where it is bitterly cold. The sudden transition makes for great humor.

Wanting to minimize the risk to my show, I inserted my white-water rafting segment immediately after the bit about the hot beach. I told my subjects, "Now that we have plenty of suntan lotion on, we are ready to go on a trip – a white-water rafting trip on the Colorado River!" At that point, the people on stage proceed to put on helmets and life jackets. Then, they strap themselves in, pick up imaginary paddles, and start rolling down the Colorado rapids that exist in their minds. The trip is made complete with a temperamental captain, and a number of tour guides and translators for the tourists on board. It concludes when the river unexpectedly leads to Niagara Falls on the horizon and the crew has to row backward frantically.

When the bit ends, my volunteers feel as if they are completely soaked from the rapids and find themselves instantly transported to Alaska, having to huddle and rub the shoulders of the person next to them to keep warm. The whole routine is great fun and always gets lots of hearty laughs.

This skit is very special to me not only because I wrote it, but because it was a challenge that I faced and solved. More than that, it demonstrates exactly what can be accomplished when you are not afraid to take the so-called "impossible" tasks head-on and have confidence in your own abilities.

Perception Is Everything

It is incredible the way our understanding can influence the things we see and interpret. Often, what we think we are witnessing from the outside is something altogether different.

One of my daily habits is to get out of bed and walk over to my bedroom window when I first wake up. I like to see what the day outside has in store for me, especially when it comes to the weather. Once, on a particularly bright, sunny morning, I saw my neighbor walking his dog. It was the kind of serene, picturesque setting you only see in the movies. The air was clear and fresh dew was on the ground. Flowers were blooming, birds were chirping, and squirrels were busy taking acorns and other treats back to their nests.

It was no wonder, then, that my neighbor seemed very much at ease. He had a leash in his hand, and was enjoying a leisurely stroll alongside his best friend, with the dog leading the way. Neither of them seemed like they were in particular hurry to get anywhere. In fact, my neighbor had his headphones on, and seemed to be enjoying the soundtrack to his outing.

I have always been fascinated by the way music can influence us. It really does "push our buttons," energizing our bodies and minds in unexpected ways. On more than one occasion, I have seen people joyously and spontaneously break into dance for no apparent reason, only because they love a certain beat or melody. There is something magical about the way a set of sounds can be interpreted by our minds and bodies.

This seemed to be one of those occasions. As I was looking on – unseen by my neighbor – I noticed his face change shape. He looked to be singing along to the track, enjoying the music so much that his whole body bent out of shape and started rocking. I had no idea what kind of music he preferred, but I was starting to become curious. As I saw it, anything that could be so moving just *had* to be worth listening to. In my mind I heard pianos, violins, or maybe even drums and electronic instruments.

From my vantage point, behind the closed window, his spontaneous joy was something like a minor miracle. It brought a big smile to my face. What I could not understand, however, was that my neighbor's spontaneous dancing was not jump-started by a piece of music… instead, a spider had left a web between two branches in his path, which he had inadvertently walked into.

Perception is the key to evaluating any situation. My lack of knowledge about what was really going on allowed me to make assumptions that were ultimately incorrect. Every situation in life needs to be assessed from different angles. Context matters. If you cannot see what is going on from different points of view, and observe without prejudice, you might find yourself dancing to a tune that is not really there to be heard.

Welcome to Comedywood

On my 30th birthday, I arrived home from a long trip feeling both exhausted and elated. I had just finished a week of sold-out shows in Texas, performing three times each night. I was looking forward to some quiet time at home, but was surprised to find my mother at the airport to pick me up instead of my new wife.

She explained that Daphna had been busy. Jetlagged as I was, I did not really think much about it. Besides, I have never been one to make a big deal of my birthday. We get older every day, so why celebrate one of them instead of another?

When I finally got home, I found the real reason for my new bride's absence – our apartment was filled with friends and family members who were all eagerly awaiting to scream "Surprise!" when I arrived. I had not expected a thing. As tired as I was, I could not help but appreciate the time and effort it must have taken her to gather everyone who mattered to me in the world together in one place.

In the midst of the party, I mentioned to a friend that things could be a lot simpler if I had a comedy club of my own. It would mean much less travel to get into a car and head across town instead of constantly being on the way to the airport to board a plane. It was not just idle chat; the idea had been growing in my mind for some time.

The years I spent touring around North America did not just make me a better comic; they gave me a chance to see how the best clubs and venues operated. I was always curious about the other side of the business, and had developed a habit of asking many questions of the owners, managers, and bookers I worked with. Over time, I developed a good sense of what it took to run a successful comedy club, with the dream of owning my own place someday.

In addition, my wife's brother Doron had been talking about opening up a restaurant for a long time. It seemed like his vision could come together with mine, and we might be able to turn our ideas into a reality at some point. I explained this to my friend, who surprised me by saying his father had a building that had just become vacant, and that we could rent it fairly inexpensively. We decided to check it out.

Ultimately, the location did not end up being right for our needs, but our visit turned out to be the spark that transformed our shared daydream into a concrete goal. Together, my brother-in-law and I began a wide search that ended with a large space on the corner of Bathurst and Steeles in the north end of Toronto. It was in an old neighborhood, and there was nothing like it around for miles. We felt certain we could make the location and concept work.

After putting together a business plan, we visited the bank and secured $450,000 in financing. We negotiated a lease, hired an architect, and set ourselves on the task of designing a top-rate comedy club.

I knew the entertainment business, while my brother-in-law was familiar with food operations from years spent working in restaurants. I also involved my best friend, Ofer, who had lots of experience in the food service world and signed on as manager. I dreamed of having my own stage to perform on, and being able to provide a venue for up-and-coming talent in Toronto. I also felt sure I could use my network of agents and performers to draw in great acts.

That dream was well on the way to becoming a reality, but there were a few snags along the way. Building codes stipulated we had to build new exits to accommodate our capacity of 383 people. There were lots of smaller logistical considerations, too. For instance, you will never realize how much inhaling and exhaling a few hundred individuals can do until you start looking at different codes and ordinances. In order to comfortably host that many, we had to put a large air-conditioner on the roof to handle exhaust. Then, there was the long and detailed process of applying for a liquor license.

It seemed as if every time I turned around, there was a new challenge. One of them still remains vividly in my mind. One day, after workers had dug up a floor in order to put in pipes for the bar and washrooms, we heard a cricket chirping in those trenches in the middle of the night. I became slightly obsessed with getting rid of them. What would happen if, in the middle of some unfortunate comic's performance after they delivered a punchline, they heard *actual* crickets?

Eventually, the project got close to completion and we had to decide on a name. Many different options came to mind. I wanted the name of the club to reflect what was happening there, and preferred a one-word moniker that related the idea that we were "Hollywood North," presenting top touring comics and variety acts. Thus, Comedywood was born. Opening night was November 23, 1995.

Being a Good Neighbor

The Toronto comedy scene at that time had only a few venues: Yuk Yuk's, Second City, and the now-defunct Laugh Resort. I felt very confident that a city with more than two million people could benefit from an additional comedy club in the suburbs, where I had grown up. The venue could fill a void, and act as a banquet hall in the neighborhood for private and corporate events.

I knew from my experiences on the road that there were politics involved when competing comedy clubs opened and operated in the same market. So, in order to smooth the way for our success, I got in touch with the other club owners before we ever opened to extend a friendly greeting from which our relationships could grow. I wanted to distance myself from the notion that we were infringing on their territory, and to let them know our comedy format was going to be drastically different from theirs. We were going to become colleagues in the suburbs, not competitors doing business across the street.

What set Comedywood apart was that our club acted as a dinner theater, serving food and presenting acts that ranged from comedy to magic and hypnosis. We concentrated on bringing in performers who had a universal appeal. Being in the suburbs, I wanted patrons to be able to bring whole families to a show without having to worry about the content or appropriateness of a given act.

Much of the comedy being performed downtown was raw and uncensored. It was not unusual for audience members to avoid the front row because they were afraid of being picked on. I did not want that kind of vibe in my club. It had to be family-friendly and inviting. This proved to be a bit of a challenge at first. I had more than a few inexperienced comics storm out of the club, telling me, "If I cannot swear, I will not work here." In response, I simply showed them the door.

Part of this was based on principle. It was my house, so they had to abide by my rules. And I did not want to lose my customers. I also felt, however, that young comics benefited from that approach. Many of them did not know how to work clean without being able to rely on the crutch of swear words and blue humor, which are ways to get cheap laughs. I made exceptions for my headliners, who were never censored. After all, I figured they were seasoned pros and knew the strengths and weaknesses in their own acts. The majority of them paid back my trust by providing clean material and lots of laughs.

Each night featured three or more performers, and we made a big effort to have developmental spots on the bill to help grow local talent. The structure was to introduce a master of ceremonies, followed by a feature act, and to finally present a headliner. This was very similar to the way comedy was presented in America, with the middle spots in the show used to develop young comedians. They were not paid much, but could get stage time, experience, and the chance to work on new material.

As a result of that philosophy, I am proud to say that I have been instrumental in giving stage time to some of the biggest stars working today. A few moved on to stage and screen, while other comics who worked my club have had brilliant standup careers and have appeared at top venues around the world.

Homegrown Talent

In those first few days, I tapped into my network of friends in the business. Some were comics I knew who needed work, while others were ready for the challenge of becoming a headline performer but had not been given the chance. They just needed time on stage, and to develop a bit more material. I always had a knack for recognizing potential in others, and seeing who had the drive to succeed. I had been through the same experience myself, and wanted to help some rising stars make their way up in the business.

One of the first comedians I brought into the club was Ralphie May, a big guy with an oversized persona and talent to match. We had worked together on the road many times, when he had served as my opening or feature act. On several occasions we had appeared one after the other at the Comedy Showcase in Houston, where he lived at the time and where I performed regularly. We've been good friends ever since, and you might recognize him as the runner-up on the first season of the TV show *Last Comic Standing*.

Ralphie was ready to be a headliner, but as is often the case, a newer performer will sometimes have better success on the road than at home. And so, he hadn't yet gotten the chance to be a headliner in Houston, where he lived and performed all the time. Once Comedywood opened, I gave him the chance to shine.

There was only one problem – being the rather large individual that he is, Ralphie was unable to fly easily or economically. In order to work at our club, he actually drove from Houston all the way to Toronto. To make it worthwhile, I booked him at the club for three weeks. I will never forget how, the day before his very first headlining gig, Ralphie was helping us bring in beer and bottles, because our liquor license had been approved that very day. These days, he is a superstar and a big name in the industry. I can only say that the success could not have come to a better person.

As much as I wanted to support local up-and-coming comics, I did not have time to meet with all of them and provide coaching. So I brought in a local comedian, Adam Pal, who was already running an independent open mic on his own. He liked to combine humor with his guitar, and was popular across Toronto. I saw the same determination in him that I had felt in my own career. Adam was eager to learn and perform, and his comedy had an edge. On stage, he brought laughs, and away from the spotlight he was constantly in my face with boundless energy and a seemingly never-ending supply of ideas and questions.

Whenever big names came through town to perform at our club, I gave Adam and his roster of up-and-comers spots on the show to help them grow their careers. He made the most of his Comedywood stage time, and eventually performed in faraway places like Las Vegas and Hong Kong.

Adam became my right hand in the club for many years, often handling comedians and bookings for me. We used to argue, good-naturedly, about how things should be done. I jokingly fired and then re-hired him on a daily basis. He is as funny and hard-working as anyone you will ever meet in life, and the fact that he made it to the top does not surprise me in the least. When I last checked, he was serving as a producer on a TV show called *Out There* with Melissa DiMarco.

The Home Front

Comedywood took up a lot of my time and energy, but it was far from the only thing going on in my life. At the same time that the clubs were taking off, I was still working as a full-time performer, doing upward of 300 shows a year. Some were on my own stage, but many were spread throughout North America. Between managing my own schedule, booking talent to appear at both venues, and overseeing the day-to-day business side of things, I also aspired to be a good husband and father.

My wife and I decided to grow our family almost immediately, and I was soon blessed with two gorgeous little girls. I often think that, in those early years, the two of them grew up on my lap while I was using the computer or talked on the telephone. There was always more work to do, but I felt my main priority was to be a good father. I loved spending time with them. Often, after a stint on the road, I threatened to wake them up in the middle of the night just to play.

Luckily, I had a lot of time to work from home. So, even though my girls knew Daddy sometimes went away to work, they also got to spend time with me around the house. I played with toys, built forts with pillows, dressed up with them, helped fill in coloring books, and sang songs from children's TV shows in between looking over receipts for the club, making calls to agents, and otherwise trying to stay on top of my multiple careers. It was a busy time, but also one that was filled with lots of joy, laughter, and immense feelings of love for my children.

In the midst of all this, Comedywood was doing very well. My own appearances were selling out, and we were bringing in top entertainers from across North America. In a relatively short amount of time, we paid off all of our business loans and were turning a healthy profit. Seeing a prosperous future on the horizon, I decided it was time to buy a house. I had two small children, and wanted a nice place for them to grow up. When we found the perfect house, it was a bit expensive for the money I was actually making, but I was confident everything was going to continue in an upward trajectory.

Because the home had been recently built, it required constant updates and little bits of fine-tuning. Our home had two entrances: one at the front and one in the back. There was a doorbell at the front door, but deliverymen liked to use the back entrance, located just off the garage, to drop off packages. There was no doorbell there, so I never knew whether someone had arrived unless I happened to look outside at just the right moment.

To deal with this annoying problem, I decided to install a new doorbell. However, our home's wiring did not go all the way to that part of the house. At the hardware store, I found a doorbell that was powered by a battery. When pressed, it transmitted a signal to the unit inside the house that announced each visitor with a chime. I worked on the installation well into the night, tested it until I was sure it worked, and finally went to bed at three in the morning, pleased with the results of my effort.

The next morning, I ran into my neighbor. She was in a particularly foul mood. Apparently, she had not slept all night because someone kept ringing her doorbell and running away. She went on and on about "those darn kids," but using slightly more colorful language, as I nodded my head in empathy. I did not have the heart to tell her what I figured out mid-conversation – our doorbells worked on the same frequency and my testing had led to an inadvertent prank that kept her awake through the night.

Mr. Tech

Spending more time around the house was good for my family life, but it also yielded some unexpected business benefits. With my background in computers, I was always one of the first to adopt new technologies. In fact, my wife (who often served as an assistant business manager and travel agent for the club) often worked side by side with me on a PC of her own.

This was at a time when computers were really starting to change the way people lived and viewed the world. Things like borders, time zones, and area codes that had seemed so important before were beginning to fade away into the background. All at once, laptop computers and cellphones took over the world. Suddenly, you could send a message to anyone, anywhere, even if you happened to be sitting at your kitchen table or working from a hotel room.

One of my first uses for the Internet was to connect with other comics and bookers, many of who belonged to a USENET group called alt. comedy.standup. The members were early adopters of technology who liked to trade ideas and use what they had learned to get bookings. It was a way for all of us to commiserate with one another, and to share different insights into the business of comedy, not to mention strategies for staying sane on the road.

Message boards included communications from those at all levels of the standup community, along with writers, bookers, and even some comedy fans. Professionals like Suzy Soro, Louis CK, Jim Slotek, Mark Matusof, Steve Marmel, Steve Gelder, Doug Stanhope, Bill Kirchenbauer, Cathy Boudreau, TanyaLee Davis, and Steve Downing were among those who asked and answered questions pertinent to the business. Later, the group even created a small comedy festival, Wired for Laughs in Los Angeles, that acted as an offline get-together. Unfortunately, I was unable to attend due to touring conflicts.

At the same time, I was starting to recognize the Internet, and especially search engines, offered a huge world of opportunity for comics and entertainers like myself. It is easy to forget now, but there was a time when half a dozen different search engines were all very popular. However, I built a website and configured it to be most visible on Google, because I considered it the best option available.

As a result, there were quite a few years where a search for the word "hypnotist" brought up my name in the first position. My process was simple: Whenever someone took me out of that first position, I painstakingly changed the website code to counteract for any improvements Google had made to their search algorithms. Before long, I was back in the top spot. With each new adjustment, I compensated with fresh coding.

The art and science of appearing more often to searchers eventually became a huge part of Internet marketing, and a multibillion-dollar industry, called search engine optimization, or SEO for short. At the time, I simply called it "breaking Google."

It was a very effective strategy. As the Internet became more and more widespread, and audiences started surfing the World Wide Web, I got into the habit of regularly mentioning my website address after shows and in media interviews. I often added at the end that, if fans or listeners could not remember where to find my website, they should just "Google me."

Shortly after, when online press release services started popping up, I put one out with the title "Incredible Boris Says Google Me." Apparently, I was the first person to come up with that phrase, all the way back on April 13, 2004. As a consequence, I am often credited as being the originator of that everyday term.

But lots of things in life will come around full circle if you let them. In December 2011, Google hired me to perform at their holiday party. The employees in attendance were an artistic and enthusiastic group, filled with many terrific hypnotic subjects. It was exciting to be around so many brilliant minds who have crafted the technology we all love. I hope to get the chance to work with them again in the future.

Becoming a Part-Time Superhero

Having kids has been a wonderful joy in my life, and a great way of staying grounded. Like any parent, I want to provide my daughters with more opportunities than I had in life. My meager beginnings gave me a glimpse of what it is like to want things without having the means to get them. I hope my girls will not struggle quite so much, and that I will have given them the strength they will need to make good decisions on their own. They will have to make their own mistakes and learn through experience, like we all do, but as a parent you want that to happen without any kind of serious harm or pain.

All parents want to bring our children joy without over-protecting them. In the process, we sometimes tell little white lies. As important as honesty is, it can be fun to indulge in little stories and traditions, especially when our kids are young. Later, reason and experience will take over. But when you have little ones in your house, they will accept your expertise on just about any given topic. They are like good hypnotic subjects in that way – whatever you tell them, they will believe.

I remember having to endure a stern letter delivered to the tooth fairy after she did not get the chance to place a coin under my daughter's pillow on the right night. As I recall, the tooth fairy might have been catching a redeye flight back from some far-flung destination, but that is not something a five-year-old will know or understand.

Aside from the little things like that, though, being a parent gives you a chance to be a hero. In some cases, literally so. When the movie *The Incredibles* came out, my daughters loved it. It was the animated story of a pair of retired superheroes who are called back into action, recruiting their kids (who also have superpowers) for a special mission.

Being known as "Incredible" for years, I admitted to my daughter I was a secret superhero, as well. My power was to hypnotize people. My four-year-old asked a few questions about this, and it became a secret bond between us. I even got my best friend, Ofer, to get in on the act. He went as far as to show her his cape and boots, which in reality were left over from a Halloween costume.

Masquerading as a "superhero" was lots of fun, and gave me a chance to bond with my kids. If you are a parent, you undoubtedly have done something similar.

I bring this up not to just share a fun story, or make you think I have a delusion that makes me believe I have extraordinary powers. Instead, I want to point out that we *all* deal in exaggeration and imagination. We project ideas to our kids, each other, and even ourselves.

When I told my daughter I was a superhero, and that she had probably inherited some of my powers, what I really wanted her to hear was a fun, positive message. I wanted her to understand the principle that guides my life, which is that YOU CAN DO ANYTHING.

Whatever you can see in your mind's eye, and move toward with your actions, you can achieve. I want to instill that belief in my daughters, and in everyone I meet – including those who come to see my performances.

When we go to the movies, we usually walk away with a bit of entertainment and the belief that what we have seen is pure fantasy. I would argue that is not always the case. In real life, *any of us* can be superheroes, even if we did not come from another planet or be exposed to radiation. The only thing it takes to achieve extraordinary acts, and play an important role in the lives of others, is a desire to make an impact and do the right thing.

Having kids taught me that you really can take on superpowers if you want to badly enough. Are you willing to develop yours?

Comedywood Takes Off

Although we had a lot of faith in our concept, I do not think any of us realized how much work, and how many details, was actually involved in running a brick-and-mortar business. It soon became apparent that we needed to hire help.

One of the first areas of concern was guest management. The club needed someone who could work behind the bar, manage lots of foot traffic coming in and out of the doors, and deal with the staff. That is a lot of duties to pack into one job, but we knew we had found the right person as soon as he walked through the door – a seven-foot-tall gentle giant named Dennis Leuzzi. He not only kept everyone calm and moving, but later became an integral part of the business when Ofer left the club to pursue a career in pharmaceutical sales.

Ofer hired a service staff of all-stars, some of whom he had worked with previously. Shannon, Karen, and Corey were the lifeblood of our club, and they all had very different styles. Corey and Karen took orders quietly, and then delivered food and drinks almost instantly. Shannon, on the other hand, essentially *told* customers what they wanted, took orders in rapid succession, and brought out drinks for everyone who had ordered at the same time. I can still remember the way she often wore a brace on her tray-carrying hand to support all the weight. These ladies did all the work that needed to be done in the dark, and quietly, while the show went on.

Even with a professional staff, managing service in a comedy club is not easy. That is because lots of people arrive hungry and thirsty at the same time. We needed to figure out a system to enter drink and food orders faster, so customers could be served more expediently and staff members could spend less time walking from one station to another. With every step our servers took between one location and another, the club was losing money because new orders could not be taken and processed quickly enough. We considered hiring more wait staff, but ultimately determined they would just get in the way of one another and make more noise that distracted patrons from the acts on stage. So we decided instead to put in a touchscreen computer system.

This was quite forward-thinking at the time, but it got the job done. The wait staff swept through tables to take orders, punched them into screens located right in the showroom, and knew they came out through quiet printers in the kitchen and bar. Everyone got what they needed faster, service improved, and sales went up.

As we got the business end of things straightened out, guests took notice and revenue started to grow. Still, we were largely ignored by the press. Initial reviews and media about Comedywood had a snide edge to them, making references that our club was "located at the edge of the universe" because it was not downtown. On another occasion, I ran into a reporter at a social function and asked him why he did not mention our new comedy club in his paper. He replied that he would mention us in his column if we were still around after six months, implying that we would fail long before then. I should note that even after that time had passed, he still declined to print at all about our venue or its success.

Despite the general lack of coverage, though, a few writers who followed comedy did take the time to check us out. Jim Slotek, a writer for the Toronto Sun, loved comedy and wrote about a good show regardless of where it had been put on. He provided regular commentaries. So did

Daryl Jung, a great writer with artistic integrity. He was a "downtown guy" and did not drive, but visited the club whenever we had a worthwhile act in town and we would send someone to pick him up from the bus station.

The sense we got, however, was that if we were going to get the word out, we had to do it ourselves. So we did. We promoted every show and event, and the club's popularity grew. In fact, things were going so well that we decided to add a new location closer to the heart of the city.

Going Downtown

With Comedywood full almost every night, our business was set to expand. We found a location in downtown Toronto, and started making plans to add an additional venue. Because of the experience of setting up our first club, things went more smoothly the second time around. The process was relatively inexpensive, and moved a lot faster.

The expansion made a great deal of business sense. Not only did it open us up to new markets, but it was more economical to bring in acts for two weeks at a time, rather than just paying them for a single week. For the comedians, it meant more money without having to pay for additional travel. And for us, it meant more exposure, a larger audience, and bigger ticket sales. In the press, we differentiated between our two clubs by calling them our "uptown" and "downtown" locations.

When the downtown club opened, our first headliner was Mitch Hedberg, who I felt carried an urban feel and attitude. He had a reputation of being a great comic, and I loved his stage persona.

Although he was a relative unknown to the public at the time, Mitch was already getting rave reviews within the industry for his on-stage work. When I hired him, he was slated to perform at the Just for Laughs Festival in Montréal later in the summer. Being booked for that event was and still is considered a huge stepping-stone in a comic's career. A good show there can lead to more work from agents, and even television contracts. Mitch's material blew everyone away at Just for Laughs, to the point that he signed a half-million-dollar developmental deal not long after, just before appearing at Comedywood.

As a comic, he was absolutely brilliant. His charismatic delivery had people in the audience hanging on his every word. His on-stage persona of a hippie delivering his observations in a drone-like cadence was an absolute pleasure to watch. After he was gone, local comics even imitated his delivery for weeks afterward. They were enamored with his style and personality, as was I. In spending time with him at the club, and driving him to interviews, I was amazed at the way he could move between his professional persona and likable off-stage personality.

Even then, Mitch had a bit of a reputation about his appetite for partying and drugs. But I wanted to make a splash with the opening of our second club, and to have a groundbreaking comic on stage for this new venture. So, once I knew the opening date, I booked Mitch for three solid weeks – one at our downtown club, one at the uptown location, and then back downtown again for the third week. That way, we could have a great comic to attract attention, and spend our important first nights in business concentrating on the details of our new venue, rather than worrying about whether our headliner has arrived in town for their gig.

The downtown club was located in a three-story building. There was a bar on the first floor, our comedy club on the second, and an apartment on the third. We used that living space as our comedy condo, housing out-of-town performers in a way that could not have been more convenient for them or us. To perform, they simply had to walk downstairs. And if they were hungry, we could send up food items from the first floor through an elevator that was located in the bar's kitchen. With this setup, we never had to worry too much about the logistics of getting comics from one place to another.

The first week went off without a hitch. Between shows on the second Friday night at our uptown location, however, Mitch disappeared for a while. It is not uncommon for a comic to show up immediately before their scheduled start time, so I did not worry about it too much. The show started as normal, with our emcee and featured act warming up the crowd.

As time went on, however, it became apparent that Mitch was not going to be ready to take the stage on time. I signaled to our emcee that he should "stretch" – that is, tell more jokes until the next person could get ready – and started looking for my headline act.

When I found him, he was in handcuffs being led into the club by a policeman. Apparently, a couple of fans from the first show wanted to share a joint with him in the alley behind our club. A police squad car happened to be driving by on a regular check of the neighborhood at that moment. The officers saw him smoking drugs and arrested him on the spot.

My first thought was: "How is he going to do the show?" The law enforcement professionals were not very understanding about my concerns. Despite my pleas that I had several hundred people in the audience, and my headline act in handcuffs, they were determined to toss their suspect in jail and throw away the key. I had to make a quick decision. Seeing no better way out, I gave Mitch his bail money and filled in as the headlining act myself that night.

Luckily, Mitch got through the ordeal and continued his act for the rest of the week. The charges were dropped, and the issue stayed out of the local papers. Unfortunately, his struggles with addiction did not go away so quietly, and he sadly passed away in 2005. His material was so timeless and insightful that you still see it being quoted all over the Internet today. I can only say that I am glad to have met him and seen him in action. As a comic and a person, he was truly one of a kind.

The Challenges of Working with Talent

In the years after my comedy club opened, I got to bring in lots of huge marquee acts. Pauly Shore, Tommy Chong, Wendy Liebman, Richard Lewis, Bobcat Goldthwait, Tommy Davidson, Pablo Francisco, and Jackie Mason all graced my stage and kept audiences buzzing. Eventually, this led to more attention from the press, more customers, and even more big names signing up to serve as headline acts. From time to time, I took the stage myself, and I am proud to say that I held my own as a draw for audiences.

Still, as I am sure any comedy club owner could tell you, bringing in performers meant getting interesting stories and more than a few headaches. For instance, we once had a comedian who crossed the border into Canada without obtaining the proper visa or paperwork. Even worse, he joked about the crime during a radio interview at the beginning of the week. Before long, we received a call from border patrol authorities who heard the interview and checked their records. They advised us that our comic was in the country illegally, and that it was in our best interests to send him back to get the necessary papers. He eventually did so, and was permitted to perform.

On another occasion, an American comic was stuck at the airport because immigration control had noticed he had a misdemeanor drunk driving charge as a teenager in the United States. He had been out joyriding with some friends. It was not a big deal in the States, at the time, but was considered a major criminal offense in Canada. I had to vouch for him and persuade the border guards to let him into our country to do shows.

In another case of small national differences, police once brought a comic back to the club after a night of drinking. They had stopped him in the parking lot before he could drive away. He had insisted he only had a few drinks, not realizing that Canadian beer had a much heavier alcohol concentration than what he had been used to drinking in the United States.

A certain big-name act (whom I will not identify here) disappeared between two shows on a slow night, only to return as he was about to be announced on stage. It turned out he had visited a strip club in the meantime. How he found the time to get there, have a few drinks, and make it back for his next performance was a mystery.

No recollection of big names would be complete without the kinds of eccentricities and minutia you hear about in the media. For instance, when Jackie Mason came to town, his contract rider specified certain food items that needed to be available before he performed. So I had to have a member of my staff drive to Buffalo, New York, to secure a few of his favorite snacks that were not available in Canada. After the performance, we went back into the green room and found he had barely touched them.

For all the oddities of working with comics and celebrities, though, most were a pleasure to do business with and be around. Our staff often stayed late into the night after shows to have a drink with the performers and talk with them about their lives. During these sessions, many great friendships were formed, and lots of stories were shared.

I wish I could tell them all here, but some stories are better left out of print to protect both the innocent and the guilty…

Comics Behind the Scenes

I think I have an interesting perspective on comedians. Not only am I working comic myself, but a keen observer of people who has had the chance to hire and work with hundreds of them.

What I have learned along the way is that comics are a special breed. They are willing to voice their issues or concerns to all of society for little or no money until they've built up an act. They are perfectly happy to pay their dues with no promise of success at the end. In fact, many struggle mightily before their voices are heard by the masses, and some are never really heard at all.

Comedians do not just tell jokes, though – they are the observers of our society, relating stories and views most of us only think about… and occasionally points of view we might not have bothered to think about without their help. Because they have to deliver these points in a clever and engaging way, they work on their stage personas endlessly until those traits and styles resonate with crowds. Once they know who they are on stage, and what their character is like, they begin to write material specifically for that voice.

In that way, honing an act is an immense challenge, somewhat like raising a child. It takes a lot of perseverance, and just as much luck. Nearly everyone who has seen a comedian perform thinks it is an easy job. Many people who have never taken the stage think they could do it just as well. But, while reciting a few jokes is easy, telling stories in a manner that an audience member can relate to, and that elicits a response, is a challenge and an art form all its own.

Even when comics are not performing, they are usually still thinking about new bits. In fact, on any given night you can visit the back of a comedy club and find performers diligently writing new jokes or set lists on scraps of paper or cocktail napkins. They never stop searching for the next subject of ridicule, or admiring each other's ideas. Usually, the heart of any good joke or premise is finding an unusual point of view. The best comics excel at this because of their backgrounds and personalities. Fans who meet their favorite comics away from the stage are often surprised to find they are not the most sociable people. They might not even be funny in normal conversation. That is because they tend to be outsiders who simply found a voice for their unique thoughts.

These traits only become more prevalent as comics spend a lot of time traveling from one city or venue to another, doing endless radio and television interviews at odd hours. As a result, they usually find themselves feeling most comfortable with others who have endured the same trials and tribulations. They like to hang out with other comics. Sometimes, the conversations they have with one another might seem crude, or even shocking, to outsiders. It isn't that they are terrible people, but that they are used to pushing the boundaries of what is acceptable in speech and expression. They are always looking for a new way to make a point. If that way can lead to guaranteed laughs on the stage, or at least give the audience a surprise, then all the better.

Within the world of comedy and performance, uniqueness and originality are king. In fact, the basic rule of being funny is to follow a "fish out of water" principle, which is simply to provide a new take on an otherwise common observation. These perspectives, and the stage personas that go with them, are fiercely protected because they have been developed over many years of trial and error.

One of the worst things one comedian can call another is a "hack," which is a term for a person who steals someone else's material premise and uses it in their own act. Unfortunately, in the digital age, it is incredibly easy for someone to see a video online and present the jokes or material they find as their own in the hopes that no one will ever notice. I always tried to avoid comics who stole or recycled other people's material, of course, but I have been fooled before.

For as much as comedians can be creative geniuses, many of them are terrible at the business side of things. This might be because of the conditions they work in. Most are their own bosses, can drink at work if they choose, and only get to perform their material for a short period of time. The rest of the day, they are usually traveling or writing. That leaves a lot of free time, and for some, a sense of loneliness or loss of direction. Maybe that is why drugs are an unfortunate aspect of show business, and why many comics get lost to addiction while seeking creativity and stress relief.

In our club, we instituted a maximum of two free drinks for comics who were working. We wanted to avoid performers getting too drunk before their time on stage. That is pretty standard for most comedy clubs, but sometimes comics will become friendly with staff and more drinks will be poured. Then, it is only a matter of time before you have an act who is slurring their words on stage. The same dynamics play out with drugs, sex, and other distractions that are always a part of the show business lifestyle. The most successful performers learn how to find a balance, and will not let any particular addiction or roadblock stop their path to success.

We all have habits, shortcomings, and even appetites for addictions that can take over our lives. They can stop us from achieving our dreams and goals. But, if we can master our compulsions, and keep our focus on what is really important, our true ambitions and better selves will always win.

As Seen on Television

If there is one thing I have learned in this life, and only one lesson you take from this book, it is that you have to make the decision to go after what you want. No one will ever advocate as passionately on your behalf, or talk up your strengths and best qualities, as you can.

Combining a simple belief in myself coupled with a dash of determination has gotten me everywhere I have wanted to go. As a case in point, there are thousands and thousands of comics and entertainers working across North America. Most of them dream of getting their "big break" on television.

Many will not ever pursue that dream because they think the competition is too stiff. Even more will be discouraged by the fact that TV producers are constantly bombarded with calls, emails, video clips, and press kits from new talent. They decide it is impossible, so they do not even try.

I knew the odds were against me, but decided that instead of shrinking back, I would do what I could to stand out in the crowd. I also made an effort to understand the way the game is played. What I learned, through several years of perseverance, was that television segment producers come and go. When you do not have luck with one gatekeeper, there is always the chance you will find success with the next. And likewise, if you can make a bit of headway with one person, there is a good chance they'll pop up again, on a different show with similar viewership, at a later time. After all, people's careers advance as well.

By understanding whom the different television producers were, and what their tastes, preferences, and agendas were like, I began to tailor my pitches to each one of them. Instead of being "another face in the crowd," I wanted to be someone they remembered – even if it took years for those efforts to pay off.

To be truthful, it *did* take years. And then years and years beyond that. When I first started sending tapes to various television programs, my friends used to tease me and say that I should just get a job at the post office because I spent so much time there. Every week, I did my best to get in touch with as many bookers as possible. I got turned down a lot, but I began to watch what they *were* putting on TV, and to develop an understanding of the way various contacts looked at segment ideas. I also kept building up more press credits and appearances so that I became more and more prominent with each new attempt.

After my appearance on *The Shirley Show*, my next big break came when I was contacted by Joe Bodolai, a local television producer, whose credits also included writing for *Saturday Night Live*. Working together with a woman named Sandra Faire, he put out a TV showcase for comedians in Canada, simply called *Comics*, that aired on CBC. It was a half-hour program that profiled a single performer, sometimes padded with comedy skits to showcase their talent, backed by personal stories and B-roll material.

I was the first and only hypnotist ever to be profiled on the program. I actually had more material than a half-hour segment allowed, and Joe approached the network to see if they could extend my show to a full hour. They declined, but we shot extra material anyway, just in case.

The process of preparing for the taping was interesting. It taught me about some of the business realities associated with television programs. For instance, a few weeks beforehand, I had to visit the CBC music library to choose some new music tracks, because the clips I normally used in my performance would have cost an enormous amount in royalties if we played them on air. Another request was that I use a statue of an angel in one of my skits. It was a staple on the set, and I wrote some new material to accommodate. Naturally, it was cut before the program ever aired.

The night before my segment was taped, I performed a show in El Paso, Texas. After that, I took a redeye back to Toronto. This was Mother's Day, May 11, 1997. Being the dutiful son that I am, I took flowers to my mom, and then got a few hours of sleep and prepared for the taping.

The performance was recorded at CBC Studios in downtown Toronto. My warm-up act was an amazing comedian named Mike Bullard. I worked together with him and his brother Pat on the comedy circuit before. Pat went on to host *Love Connection* after Chuck Woolery. Mike later hosted his own late-night Canadian talk show, the critically acclaimed *Open Mike with Mike Bullard*, that I made several appearances on as a guest. I was lucky to have Mike, with his natural comedic delivery and wonderful crowd skills, on hand that day. Feeling nervous before the show, drinking water, and pacing around behind the scenes, I asked Mike to stretch, and then spent a few extra minutes using the restroom.

Despite those initial nerves, the taping went very smoothly. The show was a success, and gave me a springboard from which I could pitch ideas to other talk shows. Like most things in life, it is easier to move ahead once you have already got a foot in the door. You become more of a known commodity, and people start to trust you more.

I was always grateful to Joe for giving me that chance, and the two of us stayed in touch over the years. We looked for different ways to collaborate together, including a handful of potential TV shows I could star in while he produced. Even when we did not have anything to work on, I enjoyed meeting with him over coffee. He told me stories about his *SNL* days, and what it was like to party with Andy Warhol at Studio 54.

Years later, Joe moved to Hollywood but felt like an outsider. For whatever reason, his previous success in the industry just did not translate in Los Angeles the way he thought it would. His opportunities dwindled, and eventually the money ran out. One winter, he committed suicide.

The Just for Laughs Festival in Montréal

Every July, agents and talent managers converge in Montréal to network behind the veil of comedy shows. To perform at the festival is considered a pinnacle of a comedy career. There is a multitude of venues hosting performances all over the city. As you may recall me mentioning, Mitch Hedberg got a developmental deal at the festival.

For audience members, the event is a great comedy extravaganza and a chance to see top comedic talent, some before they are even famous. For those of us in the industry, it is a place where deals get struck and careers advance. So I was overjoyed when I got my invitation to perform in 1998.

I was booked for two shows at a large outdoor venue. Montréal is a bilingual city, and I was endlessly amused to see my show advertised as "Boris L'Incroyable." As you might remember, I do speak some passable French, but I am not fluent enough to perform in the language. Thankfully, the spectators were able to follow along. A review in a local newspaper the next day proclaimed "the majority French-speaking audience was in for a treat when they stuck around for a delightfully funny show."

Luckily, the festivals producers took notice, and the next day there were huge signs promoting my show as English-speaking. All in all, it was a great performance. The mood was fantastic, I had wonderful volunteers, and the crowd responded to my humor with roaring laughter. In the years since, I have returned to the festival many times – performing six more shows in 2001, and also attending regularly to scout for talent as a club owner.

Howie Mandel

Even though my reputation as a performer was growing, I was not getting any closer to my next major television appearance. Still, I was determined not to give up.

Any performer faces long odds when trying to interest TV producers, of course, but things are especially tough for a hypnotist. That is because hypnosis is a strange medium that does not work as well on screen as it does in person. At a live event, audience members can *see* their friends and colleagues being hypnotized firsthand; on TV, viewers tend to assume the participants are actors and what they are witnessing is not real.

So, no matter what kind of reviews I got, my show was not considered a mainstream act. Still, I religiously sent updates and fresh video clips to every outlet I could think of, from *The Tonight Show* with Johnny Carson to *Jenny Jones, Maury*, and all of their talk show colleagues.

They say you make your own good luck with hard work. That might be true, because fate finally intervened on my behalf one night almost by accident.

It was a slow evening at the club, and I happened to be doing some work in my office. Out of nowhere, one of our cooks knocked on my door. He was out of breath. My immediate thoughts were of a fire or injury, but he had a different kind of emergency on his mind – there was some guy at the bar who wanted to get on stage. Ofer did not recognize him, but the cook did. The comedian in question was none other than Howie Mandel, who had recently changed his look by growing a mustache and goatee.

The conversation that had sent my cook into a frenzy went something like this:

Howie: "Hi. Can I get on stage to do some time?"

Ofer, in a skeptical tone: "Have you ever done comedy before, or performed at an open mic night?"

Howie, looking bemused now: "I have performed a few times."

At this point, I arrived and was able to establish Howie's identity. I was thrilled to have him do what he does best, which was go on stage.

After running through some new material, he thanked us and returned the next night to perform again. For the next few years, he dropped by every so often when in Toronto to do a new set. Howie was always great to see in person, and was always a big hit with crowds.

At the end of the night, after his appearance on our stage and on the way out, Howie was shaking hands with the staff. Adam Pal, who had become my booking assistant by that point, had a psoriasis condition that made the act of squeezing someone else's palm painful. He explained this to Howie, and offered a fist bump instead of a handshake. Years later, Howie disclosed to the world that he has a deep phobia of germs, and prefers to touch fists (thereby avoiding any germ contact) to shaking hands. I actually think Howie's fist bumping idea might just have originated that very night from a chance encounter.

In any case, it was several years later when Howie finally got his own syndicated daily talk program, appropriately named *The Howie Mandel Show*. He regularly featured variety acts, and I saw my window of opportunity. If nothing else, I figured I did not have anything to lose by sending a promotional package.

By then, I was well aware that producers receive and discard tapes and materials long before a host ever hears about the booking. I realized I did not have any advantage over anyone else, except that I had an interesting story about Howie's drop-in appearances at my club to share. So, along with my videos and press clippings, I included a quick letter about our experiences with Howie at Comedywood. I did not really expect much to come of it, but hope springs eternal.

Several weeks later, I received a phone call from Hedda Muscat, one of the show's producers. She was extremely thorough. She wanted to know what exactly I might be able to do on the program, and how much time it took to showcase my skills. She was so exacting in her queries that I felt sure I would never make it on as a guest. Still, I faxed, mailed, and answered everything I could to satisfy her concerns.

To my surprise, I was eventually contacted with a date to perform on Howie's show. The producers flew me into Los Angeles and put me up at the Burbank Hilton. Given that I had other business in the area, I decided to take a few extra days and bring my family along for the experience. What was the point in achieving that kind of victory, and having that kind of experience, if I could not share it with the ones I love the most?

I had to be on set at 8 a.m., and after a night of nervous energy I was ready to give my best performance. Hedda called the hotel early and asked if I was going to bring my family to the set. I replied that I would really love to, and she answered with some magic words I will never forget: "Then we'll send a stretch limo." After several decades of performing, I was about to get the Hollywood treatment!

Taping was not set to begin until 2:30 p.m., so I figured I had a world of time. But upon arrival at the set, I was whisked away to deal with a myriad of different tasks. I needed to do everything from signing paperwork to selecting audience members who could serve as hypnotic subjects for my portion of the show. Because my appearance segment needed to be fast-paced, I hypnotized some of them beforehand and then placed them back in the audience. Their hilarious responses were going to be triggered by key words that I implanted in their minds.

Howie was a wonderful host, and knew how to weave comedy into any moment that seemed to lack excitement. My portion of the program went off without a hitch, and my volunteers kept the fun going by running around the studio anytime a specific word was mentioned. I even had them interacting with the two other guests on the program, Illeana Douglas and Arsenio Hall.

Having already ridden a stretch limo to a TV show set, I decided to try to scratch another item off of my Hollywood bucket list. Being a huge Johnny Carson fan, I had always aspired to get the "OK" sign from Johnny himself. Unfortunately, the great entertainer had already retired by that point. However, *The Howie Mandel Show* was taped at NBC Studios in Burbank – even in the same studio where Johnny Carson had hosted his show for so many years. During a commercial break, I asked Howie if he would be comfortable giving me the "OK" sign in Johnny's place if he felt I was doing well. He understood completely, having once gotten the gesture from Johnny himself when he was an up-and-coming comic. So, just before a commercial break, Howie looked my way and made the sign with his hand. I was in heaven.

If the taping itself was a magnificent experience, the aftermath was even better. That episode got great ratings, and I was invited for a return appearance a month later. This time, I was given more on-air minutes to work with, and a greater degree of creative freedom.

Upon arrival to a production meeting before my second appearance on the show, I discovered that Howie was toying with a new invention – camera glasses, which could be used as a hidden camera to film in public without anyone being aware. A producer wore the glasses, which filmed everything that happened through a pin-sized lens in the center of the rims. Using a wireless signal, the resulting video was sent to a recording advice. It was perfect for Howie's sense of humor, because he could use it to disguise himself and capture interactions with the public without having them be aware of whom he was. In fact, he later used these glasses for pranks on other television shows.

Howie offered me to use the camera glasses to film one of my segments. I devised a fun way that we could take advantage of the technology. I hypnotized a handful of volunteers to eat everything in sight on my command. Using a hidden camera format, we took my subjects into a supermarket, where they started sampling foods from other people's baskets. The reactions from the un-hypnotized shoppers were priceless. Not everything could be put on air, as some of the prank victims were not that happy about what had transpired and did not sign release forms. Still, the resulting footage made for some great TV entertainment.

With the success of my two segments, it seemed likely that I was going to be invited back for a third time… or possibly even become a regular on the show. Unfortunately, *The Howie Mandel Show* was canceled after that season. I would have to find a new way in.

Montel Williams

In show business, or any business, relationships are everything. If you work hard for people and establish the right kind of reputation, they'll bend over backward to help you in return. The key is to work hard and gain someone's trust. You have to let them know you will deliver what is required and exceed their expectations.

This is important to remember when pursuing your success, and it is also the perfect way to illustrate how I used my appearances on Howie's canceled TV show to get my next big media break. After his program ended, I noticed that the executive producer, a smart lady named Diane Rappaport, was now spearheading *The Montel Williams Show*.

Using what I had already learned, I sent her a set of customized promotional materials and made numerous phone calls to ensure they got seen. I wanted very much to be considered for a guest appearance, and was armed with the knowledge that one of the key decision-makers in the process was already familiar with my work. I felt confident she noticed my professionalism, and knew I could bring in ratings. Much to my delight, she was amenable to my pitch and passed along my queries to the right producer to have me appear on the program.

I flew in early for the taping. This is partly because I did not want to rush through the network's paperwork process again, and partly because the producers wanted me to present my routines live in the studio beforehand – for blocking purposes. Blocking simply refers to the practice of getting the director and crew familiar with what a performer is about to do, so camera operators, sound people, and others involved in the production of a program can be ready to capture them. It is just like watching a rehearsal. For instance, when they saw how people reacted to being hypnotized, they could be ready to capture movements, facial expressions, and other details during the actual live taping.

Also, it gave us a chance to discuss my routines, and which ones could be tweaked for broadcast or removed altogether. We even pre-taped segments at locations around town where I could take hypnotized volunteers and unleash them on unsuspecting bystanders, similar to the way I had done on *The Howie Mandel Show*.

On the day of taping, I arrived at the studio with my wife. Daphna has been my best professional sounding board, always giving me feedback without sugarcoating her impressions. Often, she has shared an invaluable perspective at important moments, and gotten me to think about scenarios I might have otherwise overlooked. Not only do I trust her intuitions and opinions completely, but it is a treat being able to share your biggest accomplishments with someone you love.

The two of us were sitting in the green room when Montel arrived. After some quick introductions and pleasantries, he asked if I spoke Russian. I mentioned that I speak fluently, having been born in Moscow and spent many years of my childhood there. As a former military intelligence officer, he had also learned the language. And so, the two of us had a very nice conversation in my native tongue.

After our chat, I figured he would want to wrap things up and get the show started. However, much to my surprise, he asked my wife to leave the green room so he could address me in private. Once the door was closed, his semi-serious demeanor changed. With a smile, Montel switched back to English and told me that he had gone over the script and felt it was too stiff and dry. He asked me: "How are you at improv? Can you think on your feet?" I pride myself in coming through in the midst of challenging situations, and had faced many interesting and unexpected obstacles in my years performing on stage. I confidently answered that I would be able to handle anything.

At this, Montel grinned again: "Then get ready to play."

We had a lot of fun, and the taping went very smoothly. Between the in-studio segments, we showed bits that had been filmed throughout the different locations around New York City. In one scenario, we went to a supermarket where I hypnotized a person to talk to fish in the display window, believing they could talk back to them. In another, a hypnotized subject was taken to a novelty store, where she simply could not get enough of dressing up and putting on makeup. By the end, she looked like a cartoonish version of a showgirl, covered in bizarre colors and feathers, while walking the streets of Manhattan believing she was a celebrity. In a more practical segment, I helped a longtime smoker to give up the habit. She went on to discuss her experience with Montel in the studio.

As always, not everything we filmed made it on the air, due to considerations of time and corporate sensibilities. But everyone got a good laugh and my website was displayed at the end of the broadcast so viewers could find out more about me. Because the program was syndicated, it appeared in different markets at different times around the country. I watched in amazement at the way hundreds and thousands of new visits to my webpage went up with each viewing, as new audiences saw the show and got interested in my work. That day I diligently answered more than a thousand emails that came as a result of my appearance on the show.

The Bubble Bursts

The effect of a successful appearance on such a big show was overwhelming. The producers were eager to have me back, and talked with me about filming a new episode in October. Meanwhile, the phone was ringing nonstop. I received an offer to open for Jerry Lewis one day, and was booked to perform on a Norwegian cruise that was traveling to Japan the next. A TV producer from Seattle wanted to know if I could duplicate my performance on his show, which corresponded with an offer to headline at Giggles in Seattle for a week. The calls and opportunities went on and on. My comedy career had been successful before, but suddenly I had hit critical mass.

And then, the world shifted beneath my feet. My Montel appearance aired in late summer 2001, and the 9/11 attacks on Washington and New York stunned the world. Just as quickly as those opportunities had appeared, they slipped away into nothing as countless lives were changed forever. Beyond the shock and grief of seeing so much pain around me, I had to face up to the reality that the world was not in the mood for comedy. Clients did not have the budgets, or the interest, in humor or hypnosis.

I never worked with Jerry Lewis, and never returned to the Montel show. Club dates dried up, and so did my audiences in Toronto. Businesses like ours were hemorrhaging money, and I closed the Comedywood downtown location when my landlord offered to let me out of our lease.

It was a tough time, but I absolutely refused to feel sorry for myself. I knew there were a lot of people who were suffering in a much worse way than I was. Terrorists altered lives, but not attitudes – they would not be victorious. I had been through hardships before and was determined to re-invent myself. The terror and misfortune that had come so unexpectedly was not going to keep me or the nation down – we had to rebound and thrive despite a temporary setback.

Setbacks and Comebacks

I have become somewhat of an expert on the subject of phobias. This stems from academic training and many years of extensive research done for my work on television (more on this later) and how different fears can be treated through hypnotherapy.

The biggest lesson I have picked up from studying fears, and the one I really want to share with you, is this: *We learn how to be afraid*. Children are born feeling terrified of nothing. While each of us has a natural instinct for self-preservation, fear is a learned response. More often than not, it is a response that is both natural and unhelpful at the same time. It hinders us, but it can be unlearned.

On September 11, 2001, terrorists tried unsuccessfully to instill fear in our minds. What happened instead was that people came together, bonded in our grief, and decided what we could do to make the future better. The fear was only a temporary response, and I am living proof. As I write these words on my laptop, I am preparing to board a flight. The date is September 11.

The Downward Spiral

9/11 was a turning point. Mentally, emotionally, and culturally, everything changed overnight. It was apparent at the time, and easy to see that the somber mood around North America was not going to be lifting anytime soon. Comedy was pushed far from people's minds, and they were not going to feel like laughing again for a while. The economy suffered, too, with entertainment being the first thing many families and companies cut from their budgets.

Still, we managed to keep the Comedywood uptown location running. This was accomplished partly through an ongoing campaign of flyers and coupons that kept guests coming through the door, and also with a little bit of help from a government charity casino program. At the time, the authorities allowed certain types of games and bets to be placed in large halls, like ours, to benefit nonprofits.

So once a month we reserved a few normally slow nights (Sunday through Tuesday) when gambling tables could be brought in. We provided drinks and sandwiches while charity groups took care of the gaming. As a result, we were able to cover our rent at a time when other comedy clubs and entertainment venues were feeling the strain.

But charity gaming did not turn out to be quite the bargain we thought it would be. One afternoon, while the casino was running, a gang of thugs burst through the doors to rob the place in broad daylight. They must have been staking out our club for a while, because they knew exactly what to do and where to go. Within moments, they had locked the doors from the inside, and proceeded to rob the casino cage at gunpoint. Once they had the loot, they escaped out our back entrance on foot.

It was a terrifying experience. My best friend, Ofer, who was behind the bar at the time, ended up being held at gunpoint. The same gang went on to rob several other charity casinos, too, until they were finally caught trying to invade another location across town.

A few years later, laws changed and charity casino operations were banned altogether. Suddenly, we were faced once again with the challenge of bringing customers through the door, but this time without the cushion of supplemental income. To make matters more difficult, Ofer had left the business by this point to begin a lucrative career as a pharmaceutical salesman. As tough as it was to lose him, I had to admit he had found his calling. With a bubbly personality, the gift of gab, and an uncanny knack for creating lasting relationships with his humor and friendliness, he was always bound to be a hit as a drug dealer… albeit, "the legal kind."

Dennis Leuzzi, our seven-foot gentle giant of a bartender-slash-manager, stepped in and took his place. He had become more of a friend than an employee, and I looked forward to his regular 2 o'clock calls to keep me updated with club operations. He was not just loyal and dependable, but a very kind-hearted man. I remember once during a blackout in Toronto during the dead heat of summer, I found him distributing cases of water from the club's refrigerator to thirsty people on the street.

Still, even with his help, it was getting harder to stay afloat. The comedy business had not really recovered from 9/11, and subsequent news events were making things worse. During the Mad Cow disease outbreak, customers stopped ordering hamburgers (a staple of any bar or comedy club). SARS, a disease transmitted through human interaction, prevented patrons from coming out to public places.

Even the post office accidentally worked against us, when they failed to deliver 10,000 flyers and coupons. They eventually corrected the mistake, but only after the dates on the printed offers had expired. Those promotions were vital to filling our rooms, and bringing us revenue from food and drinks. Without them, our showroom started to thin out. That was bad for business, and for the atmosphere within the club. Having 50 people in an area that seats 400 does not really make for a fantastic show, and is not conducive to spreading laughter.

Things were getting tighter, and I was sleeping very little. The club was barely breaking even, and only then with a huge amount of time and effort on my part. Comedians still needed to be paid, and so did my staff. I was able to pay them, but had to resort to working long hours *and* performing on the road to supplement my own income.

It was during this difficult period that Dennis came to me early in our service one night to say he was not feeling well. He looked weak and tired, and admitted he had been coughing up blood. I sent him home, against his wishes, with instructions to get himself to a hospital or doctor so they could get to the root of the problem. I knew something was wrong when, the next day, his regular 2 o'clock phone call never came.

I found out later he had gone straight to the hospital after I sent him home from work. They immediately checked him in and performed an operation, after which he slipped into a coma. When I came to visit him, he was on a special bed that rotated his huge seven-foot frame. His doctors were doing everything they could, but he had been more ill than any of us could have imagined.

With Dennis fighting for his life, I was left to run Comedywood almost on my own. That is not just hyperbole – we were incredibly short-staffed at the time. I can remember vividly one night when I served as the "door girl," bartender, and headliner all at once, while my wife waited tables.

In the midst of all of this, the lease on our location was coming up for renewal, and our landlord wanted to raise our rent drastically. I had a moment of realization: Although our comedy club had run and succeeded for a decade, things were only going to get tougher for at least a few years to come. I had lived my dream, but now it had become something different. I could continue to pour time and money into the venture, and make it my full-time job, or walk away on my own terms and turn my attention back to performing. And so, on a single day's notice, I decided to close it down and chase a new inspiration.

Shortly after, Dennis was taken off of life support at the hospital. He was buried in November, just a few weeks after I had closed Comedywood. People came from far and wide to mourn him and celebrate his life, including many well-known comedians. It was a tribute to the many, many people he had touched in a positive way that they came to pay their respects.

I also found out a short while later that I was being audited by the tax authorities. The government had disallowed a legitimate expense, because of the mingling of my own funds with that of my comedy club, and was assessing a much higher figure than I had anticipated. What I had done was perfectly legal, but the only person who could prove it had just passed away. I fought it, and won, but the process took years.

In the end, the decision to close Comedywood was intensely painful and difficult. It was hard to let go. Even though I had lived that dream, letting go was like saying goodbye to an old friend. I had just done both.

Instead of despairing, though, I decided to immerse myself back into my work. I revamped my website and used my knowledge of computer programming to create a first-rate online presence that sent clients, agents, and bookers coming my way. I was determined not to let the problems I had faced hold me back. Unfortunately, the hits just did not stop coming.

More Adversity

Not long after my comedy club closed and Dennis passed away, my wife started experiencing health troubles, as well. She was regularly constipated and had consulted about it with her doctor. While many doctors would have been quick to send her home with a laxative, ours was astute enough to run some tests.

The diagnosis was devastating: colon cancer.

Usually, I am able to remain calm, or least *appear* calm, when faced with a major challenge. I like to keep my cool while developing possible solutions in my mind. However, this was different. I felt like the news tore me apart in an instant. I had to gather myself quickly, though. Not only did Daphna set the tone by taking the doctor's words with incredible strength, but we had two young daughters who needed strong parents now more than ever.

Before long, my wife underwent surgery to remove the tumor. That was nerve-wracking, but the following years were even more difficult, as she had to endure additional surgeries and chemotherapy.

It was already a tough time, mentally and emotionally, and the worry about my wife's health was overwhelming. But I felt as if my most important job was to show my family strength. So even though we were burdened with a tough medical challenge, we decided to face it head-on. I did my best with my wife and our girls to keep the focus on staying positive. At times, I worried they thought I was insensitive to what was happening, but I tried to convey the notion that cancer was just another obstacle, and that we HAD to work together against it.

While Daphna was recuperating, I became a stay-at-home dad. I took a few select dates on the road to keep money coming in, but only when we had family members who could help to cover. It meant a big change of pace for all of us, but it was a sacrifice I would make a thousand times over.

To our great fortune, Daphna's doctors caught the cancer early and she is now in full remission. The episode was terrifying, but it also made me appreciate my family, and the good things in my life, even more than I had in the past.

Fail First, Succeed Later

I began this chapter by talking about fears and phobias. I pointed out they are learned, and not naturally inherited. How we think about ourselves, the world around us, and the things that happen to us greatly affects our mindset and actions.

Fear is a primal instinct. It exists to keep us safe from external dangers and impending doom. Once we become afraid, the fight-or-flight response governs our course of action. But even experiencing those emotions can feel disorienting. For that reason, it is always easier to avoid adversity than it is to face it. Most people will go on as long as possible without confronting something that scares them, or even thinking about it.

I advise you to do the exact opposite. Choose to tackle the unknown head-on. That way, you do not have to spend your life worrying about possible outcomes – just face up to whatever scares you, conquer your anxieties, and move forward. Doing so will not just make you feel better; it will give you a sense of decisiveness that is attractive to those around you. Every day, people follow leaders who speak and move with a force of purpose; girls fall in love with "bad boys" who are not afraid to push ahead to the front of the pack; moments are seized by the men and women who spend more time discovering opportunities than they do worrying about possible consequences of their actions.

No matter what you do, or how you live, you are only going to have a finite amount of time on this planet. I have never been particularly bothered about my own mortality. I worry more about my wife and daughters than I do myself. Even though death is humanity's No. 1 collective fear, as noted in one survey after another, it is a fact of life that *we are all terminal.* As strong as our self-preservation instincts are, we are better off making the most of the lives we have than worrying about what will happen when they are over.

Another fear most people have centers on public speaking. This, once again, comes down to an issue of confidence. When you can work with an audience, and transmit your passion, ideas, and wisdom to them, you increase your usefulness, make yourself a leader, and improve your own self-esteem. The fear is real, but so are the consequences of letting fear hold you back from everything you can achieve.

There are countless other examples, but what I want to instill in you is the knowledge that *there is really nothing to be afraid of.* Regardless of how you choose to live your life, some good things are going to happen, and some bad things are going to happen. What you are probably afraid of, deep down, is not the bad things, but the process of change that surrounds them.

As humans, we spend a lot of time and energy trying to avoid chaos. From a very early age, we are conditioned to fear the unknown, both by our parents and the world at large. However, adversity and change are natural parts of living. The harder we try to fight them, the more difficult we make things for ourselves. When we are decisive, instead of constantly wondering "what if," we can stop worrying about change and what might happen if we fail, and start thinking about the successful outcome of our actions.

Just as adversity is a part of life, so is failure. Many things you try to do will not work out, just as they have not for me. I have bombed in my first big stage appearance, been rejected by hundreds of agents and producers, had events interfere with the progress of my business and career. But I have also entertained millions of people, changed lives, traveled around the world, seen my dream of owning a comedy club become a reality, and known the love of a beautiful family.

Every setback is an opportunity to grow and learn. If you want to succeed, you often have to fail first. That is not just the best way to get the experience and perspective you really need, but it can make every victory that much more enjoyable. I love my wife, the success of my career, and everything else that is good in my life all the more because I have come close to losing them at times. You cannot prevent all the setbacks life has in store for you no matter how hard you work, but you can change the way you think about them and write your own story so the next chapter is a better one.

Traveling the World

As the entertainment business gradually recovered from 9/11, and I focused my efforts on performing, I was offered opportunities to perform in some interesting places around the world.

One of these trips was to the island of Bermuda. Being a big fan of documentaries, I was immediately thrilled. I knew all about the Bermuda Triangle, and of the area's natural beauty. I was also excited for the event itself – the organizer, a man named O'Brian Roberts, presented a showcase once a year that featured local magicians and a headlining specialty act like me. He took care of all the travel and visa requirements. I just had to show up, give a great performance, and have a good time.

My first couple of days involved very little free time, since there was a lot of radio, television, and online press to take care of. At one point, a local DJ named Steve Franks dared me, on air, to hypnotize him during a commercial break. After I did, we came back with a few bits and personalities I had created on the spot. In the end, I took over the disc jockey duties while playing off his hypnotized personas. This created a stir, and the local news outlet, The Royal Gazette, ended up running an article about me with a photo that covered half the page. With that bit of media attention, we were able to draw in audience members from every corner of the 21-mile-long island.

The event itself went off beautifully. It was held at the City Hall Theatre in Hamilton, and I had the honor of appearing beside O'Brian, along with local magicians Mike Bishop, Shelley Johnston, and Rich

"Richie" Lathan. There was also a talented local artist by the name of Roger Moniz, who opened the show with a dazzling display of his magical abilities. The performance was very well-received, and got a lot of media coverage.

What I remember most about Bermuda is not performing, however, but just the sense that it was an amazing place filled with friendly people. From the moment I got off the plane and started traveling toward the Fairmont Hotel, I noticed that everyone on the island seemed to know one another. Even while driving, they exchanged friendly "hellos" by simply tapping their car horns and waving.

The locals have unusual attire to go with their friendly demeanor. Bermuda shorts with knee-high socks and a jacket are regular dress, even if you are headed to work. Another local custom was the "Dark & Stormy" drink, which is a mix of ginger beer and other ingredients that carries a big kick.

I will never forget walking on the beautiful pink sand the island is famous for. As it turns out, it is actually regular sand, but with particles of broken pink reef coral mixed in to give its distinctive rosy glow. Standing at the edge of the pier and glancing into the crystal-clear waters, you can see exotic fish sporting every color of the rainbow drifting by. Some of them even jumped out of the water, as if to say, "Welcome to my world!"

Bermuda lived up to its reputation and will always have a special place in my heart.

The Vegas Strip

Sometimes, the biggest and best opportunities present themselves out of the blue. If you miss them, you will never notice. But if you keep your eyes open, these happy coincidences can come from almost anything... and end up being highlights in your career, or even your life.

That was certainly the case for me when I found myself performing in Las Vegas. As part of the promotion for the event, I was invited to appear as a guest on *The Vegas Show*, a TV program that provided viewers with a look at local issues and highlighted some of the entertainers coming through town. Regularly hosted by Brian McKnight and Sheena Easton, it was a big show in the city. It was filmed at the Golden Nugget Casino showroom, on the same stage where in years past, The Rat Pack, with Frank Sinatra, Sammy Davis Junior, and Dean Martin, strutted their stuff.

On this particular day, however, Brian McKnight was on tour. His temporary replacement was none other than Howie Mandel, with whom I was obviously already familiar. Being old acquaintances, he invited me, along with several members of the show crew, to come with him to the MGM Grand, where he was performing that night.

After his show, we all went backstage. He gave us a glimpse at a new TV program he was working on, and I spent the night hanging out with Howie and one of his friends, an incredibly talented comedian named Vic Cohen – an impromptu performer who could make any moment hilarious. Vic is always willing to go to any length to get a laugh, and later became the subject of a documentary called *Committed*, as well as appeared on Howie's different shows repeatedly.

When it came time to actually tape my segment on the show, I wanted to do something that was different and fit the Las Vegas theme. Eventually, I came up with a silly routine that got big laughs. The movie *Finding Nemo* was immensely popular at the time, and I developed a bit that combined gambling with animated sea life.

It worked like this: Upon introducing myself to a volunteer and doing a few hypnotic demonstrations, I described Las Vegas as a city filled with "whales." In gambling terms, that meant a high roller, but to those outside of the casinos, the idea that came to mind was one of a huge sea mammal. So I hypnotized my subject to believe he was speaking the language of whales, and then asked him to invite new visitors to the city. In response, he happily shrieked and squeaked as if translating my words. It was a little bit ridiculous, but viewers loved it.

Howie Mandel was not the only big-name entertainer I was surprised to run into. While in town, a friend arranged from the alt.comedy. standup online forum invited for me to attend a performance of the brilliant magic duo Penn & Teller at the Rio Hotel. She happened to be married to Mike Jones, a versatile jazz pianist who is the musical director for the pair's performance. Mike began the show by playing the piano for a well-disguised Penn, who plucked a standup bass incognito as the audience entered the showroom. This provided a wonderful initial illusion – audience members were completely unaware that the headliner was hidden right in front of them in plain view. The rest of the evening was equally as masterful, with each new trick or deception topping the last.

After the performance ended, I was invited backstage. While Penn has a big personality that matches his enormous height, his partner comes off much differently in real life than he does on stage. I spent hours talking with Teller, the usually silent member of the duo, whom I had met many years prior during one of their performances in Toronto. Even being jetlagged as I was, the conversation was enlightening. Although Teller's on-stage persona is of an angelic mute who mimes his responses, backstage he is an extremely talkative and curious individual. He was intrigued about hypnosis and asked me many different questions, including my views and experiences, surprising me with his knowledge and mastery of the subject. There are not many people you could ever meet in show business, or life, who are as immediately smart, kind, and likable.

Toward the tail end of my trip, I discovered that a new television show called *The Casino* was also being filmed at The Golden Nugget, which had served as the set for *The Vegas Show*. It was a program by the legendary producer Mark Burnett, and followed two entrepreneurs who had bought the casino property as an investment. Each episode featured stories about hotel patrons and workers, or sometimes the high rollers who came in to place big bets. It was a way to give viewers a glimpse of the trials and tribulations of owning a casino.

By chance, I happened to bump into one of the show's producers. Figuring I had nothing to lose, I suggested they included a hypnosis segment. They were intrigued, so I selected a volunteer inside the casino, with the cameras rolling, and hypnotized him to do silly skits.

Suddenly, though, we ran into a problem. According to union rules, the crew had to take a lunch break. We would not be able to resume filming for another few hours. Hypnosis can last a long time, and I trust in my abilities. But letting the subject go free in a city filled with endless distractions was a bit risky. How long could the trance last? I was not positive my segment would survive the break.

I gave him a suggestion to be back at exactly 3 p.m. Much to my relief, he showed up exactly when I told him to.

With that hiccup out of the way, I moved into what I had planned as the feature routine for my segment. In my stage show, I have a bit where hypnotized volunteers believe cocktail napkins have become $100 bills. Actually, they started as $20 bills a long time ago, but with inflation being what it is, I have had to increase the value and denomination over the years. It is always fun to see people's excitement when they think they are receiving endless wads of money. Hypnotized subjects often put the bills away in their pockets and wallets to the audience's delight. Occasionally, women stash them in their bras for safekeeping.

It is a fun premise, and I wanted to use it again for the show. So, with the cameras rolling, I sent my hypnotized subject to go gambling inside The Golden Nugget. Instead of real currency, though, he was attempting to spend the cocktail napkins he believed to be cool, crisp hundred-dollar bills, which he referred to as Benjamins. Much to his surprise, his bets were being refused again and again. Eventually, he got into a (thankfully verbal) fight with a cage boss, who patiently and politely tried to explain that my subject needed to wager with real bills. The segment ended with my volunteer complaining out loud, "Nobody will take my money in Vegas!"

Another Day, Another Desert

A few years later, I received an email inviting me to appear as a presenter at the Women as Global Leaders conference in Dubai, United Arab Emirates. Because the message began with such pleasantries as "compliments of the day to you," and mentioned the names of other well-known dignitaries scheduled to appear at the conference, I initially suspected it was spam. Performers get these all the time, and they tend to feature offers to appear at distant conferences that turn out to be nonexistent.

Luckily, I decided to do a little bit of research before I discarded the note, and found out the event really was taking place. Unfortunately, I still had to turn the date down, as it conflicted with a block of time I had set aside for a family vacation.

I had already been contracted to perform at the historic Harriet Himmel Theater in West Palm Beach, Florida. My show was booked for the Friday before spring break, so I decided to take my family away on a cruise during the week my daughters were off school. We were set to leave from Miami on Sunday, and all of us were looking forward to a wonderful getaway from the cold and snow that had been hanging over Toronto. Personally, I was excited to have a bit of time away from performing, as well. Knowing that the two dates could not work together, and that the travel logistics would have been a nightmare anyway, I politely declined and looked forward to a restful vacation.

The event organizers were not ready to give up so easily, however. They informed me that this was a royal command performance, and I was going to follow speeches by Jane Fonda and the Duchess of York, Sarah Ferguson.

Being fairly well-connected within the industry, I put in a call to Jane Fonda's publicist to verify the legitimacy of this request. After giving my credentials on the telephone, my contact did not confirm or deny anything. Instead, she simply told me, "You will receive a reply shortly." Several hours later, my phone rang with the answer: "Yes, Jane Fonda is scheduled to speak at this function."

I found myself faced with a dilemma – how to be in two places at the same time? Time with my family is extremely important to me, but I knew getting the chance to contribute to such a monumental event could be a once-in-a-lifetime opportunity, and an important step in my career.

I decided to look into flights. It was possible, via British Airways, to leave Miami on Saturday night and arrive in Dubai the following evening. Coming back, I could fly out of Dubai and meet our cruise ship in the Grand Cayman Islands on Wednesday. I could not break the laws of physics, but with careful travel planning I *could* do both by missing only the first few days of the cruise.

Communicating with anyone on the opposite side of the world is always difficult. Time differences mean phone calls have to be made in the middle of the night, and an "immediate" response can be delayed nearly 24 hours. So I was still a bit dubious that the whole thing would come off. However, once I suggested the travel agenda, I received an almost instant reply. I was simply told: "Your itinerary will be there tomorrow." Lo and behold, it was.

With the details out of the way, I started to get excited. I have always loved going on adventures, and this was definitely a way to taste the unknown and strive for new experiences. However, Mother Nature was determined to not let me off the hook so easily. Spring snowstorms are not unusual on the east coast of Canada, and some unexpected weather led to delays in my departure. I made it to Miami a little late, but still with plenty of time for my performance in West Palm Beach, which went smoothly.

I spent the following morning with my family by the pool, and headed to the airport while they packed for their cruise. My flight from Miami to Dubai departed in the evening, and I was thankful to be able to sleep on the long journey so I could be refreshed for what lie ahead.

Upon my arrival in the United Arab Emirates, a man in an orange jacket was waiting for me as I exited the plane. He whisked me past other passengers through the waiting lines for immigration and baggage claim.

My passport was stamped and I was taken immediately to a waiting car. The experience pulled me back to my days of riding to Howie Mandel's studio in a limousine. Suddenly I felt very important!

The conference was held at Madinat Jumeirah, a luxury property where the famous sailboat hotel is located. Although it was already late in the evening, conference representatives greeted me and outlined my schedule for the next two days. I was even offered a greeting cocktail – an exotic juice mixture that is common in the region, as alcohol is forbidden. While I drank it, my handlers explained several matters of etiquette to me, including how and when I could talk or interact with royalty, and what was expected of me when I did.

With those formalities out of the way, I was taken to my room, which was found in a secure wing of the hotel, reserved for high-end dignitaries and celebrities. It was exquisite, and had every amenity one could ask for. My suite overlooked the sailboat hotel Burj Al Arab, which changes colors every few seconds when it is dark. I sat on the balcony, observing the waves hitting the beach and taking in the breathtaking scenery, both natural and man-made. Tired as I was, I just could not manage to sleep yet. I was in Dubai!

On another balcony nearby, a group of people were loudly discussing matters that seemed to have great importance. With a closer look, I realized the woman sitting on the veranda a few paces away with several smartphones in front of her was none other than Sarah Ferguson, the Duchess of York. She seemed to be writing postcards and text messaging all at once. I thought of snapping a few discreet pictures to keep as mementos, but made a conscious decision not to. I knew she faced cameras all day long, and realized I should respect her individual privacy, star-struck as I was.

Later, I got a chance to say hello in person and look into her eyes. I have always believed that the eyes tell the story of a person's life. Hers related to me the sense of someone who endured and persevered through many hardships. To this day, I admire her strength and ability to deliver a positive message despite all the challenges and obstacles life can present. I think she remains a wonderful role model for young women everywhere, including my two daughters.

Eventually, I retreated to my bed and slept for a few hours so I could be ready for the long day ahead.

When morning came, my sense of wonderment had not faded. I arrived downstairs at the assigned hour, and found the fountain in the front lobby being filled with fresh rose petals by a diligent worker. My driver was also present, in a crisp uniform, waiting to take me to the venue.

I was amazed at the level of detail and planning that had gone into the event. After I was advised once again about the proper etiquette for meeting members of the royal family, the meeting planners talked with me about my show. They mapped out what would happen to the minute. Luckily, I was a veteran of the stage, and able to work within their exacting guidelines.

My performance was scheduled for the afternoon, and I was advised there was a possibility that I might be asked to perform again if the Sheikh happened to enjoy my show. If that were to happen, it was a great honor rarely bestowed on anyone, and the second performance would take place for a different audience in the evening. Additionally, the second show was for a completely different audience from the first. I love making people laugh, and replied that I of course would be happy to accept if and when the opportunity arose.

While attendees came from around the world, I was fortunate that most of my audience was quite fluent with the English language. It was mainly composed of young women, who were being primed to become leaders of the future. They seemed like a fun, energetic group, and I found myself feeling grateful that they let a male performer appear for such an audience.

I can only describe the event itself as a fantastic extravaganza. I learned that His Excellency Sheikh Nahayan Mabarak Al Nahayan was a very forward-thinking individual, and a mastermind at entertaining and engaging his guests. In addition to several members of royalty, there were many dignitaries and world leaders in attendance. For instance, I met Helen Thomas, known as the "First Lady of the press" at the White House. I also met policymakers like Carol Bellamy from UNICEF, Hubertus Hoffmann from the World Security Foundation, and esteemed scholars like Mary Sue Coleman, president of the University of Michigan.

My performance followed remarks by Sarah Ferguson and then Jane Fonda. I was a hit, and was asked to do a second performance for special guests the same night. During the VIP dinner, they showed a spectacular video and laser light presentation that delivered the message of leadership and peace. Everyone in the audience received a rosary made from real pearls. It was tough to follow such a spectacle, but I riddled my comedy show with messages of positive thinking, and specifically focused on the theme of lifting limitations. I wanted to leave the group with a sense that they could do anything they only dared to dream of.

For the next few days, I got a sense of what it was like to be truly famous. Paparazzi followed me around, taking pictures. I might be a fairly well-known performer, but appearing next to the Sheik and assembled dignitaries seemed to put me in a whole new stratosphere. Simply being invited to walk or sit next to him was a sign of importance, and made me a target for photographers.

On the second evening of the conference, guests were treated to an event in the Sahara desert. First came a traditional dinner in Bedouin tents that could only be described as a once-in-a-lifetime experience. It was like visiting an oasis mirage in the ancient Middle East, complete with handcrafted carpets lying in the sand and velvet sitting pillows that the Sheikh's staff had placed on the ground. That was followed by a performance that told the story of an Arabian king and his sons, who battled evil forces together. It featured an elaborate presentation narrated by Omar Sharif and was backed with holograms, dancers, horses, and another light and laser show.

From my involvement in the conference, I received two "Global Leader" awards I treasure. One was handed to me during a lavish presentation on stage, while the other arrived by mail shortly after I had returned home.

It was a wonderful gift, but one that presented certain logistical difficulties. I like to travel light, normally bringing only a carry-on suitcase and laptop bag with me wherever I go. The award I had been given was a sizable piece of art, made of twisted metal that was sharpened at the top. It was very easy for me to imagine how it might be used as a weapon, and I felt certain security might have a problem with me taking it on the airplane. It did come in a nice leather bag, but it definitely looked dangerous. However, I wanted to take it on board the aircraft, as I worried it could get damaged if I had to check it in with suitcases, golf clubs, and other items that might be treated roughly by baggage handlers.

Upon arrival at the airport, I went to the security station and declared my new prize possession. There was a small commotion among the staff, as they discussed something in a language I did not understand. Eventually, I saw that supervisors were being called over to deal with the situation. During this time, numerous different individuals came to meticulously examine the award for themselves.

Eventually, one of the managers asked me: "Who gave you this?" I rattled off the Sheik's long, formal name, being quite familiar with it at that point from the numerous speeches and presentations I had heard. At this, the supervisor politely handed me the award back with a simple invitation to "go right ahead."

The trip home was pleasant and uneventful. I made it to Grand Cayman Islands and met up with the cruise ship to continue with my family on our vacation. I had some elaborate stories to share with them, and an experience that I never could have expected.

As it happened, I got the opportunity to return to Dubai six months later to perform at a function for an international group of businessmen. It even included another elaborate laser and firework show. I will never forget the beauty and charm of either trip, and sincerely hope I have more such adventures ahead.

My Travel Agent

My wife is not just a great partner in the romantic sense, but also invaluable in my business. For instance, Daphna normally handles my travel arrangements, booking my flights, hotels, and cars for me. When new performances are added at the last minute, she tweaks my itineraries and adjust my routes as needed, making sure I get everywhere I need to be on time.

She also makes sure the travel portion of my job is not harder than it has to be. She puts me in exit rows on airplanes, gets me window seats when I ask, and even orders kosher meals for me (because they are usually served first). She knows just what I should say to airline employees at the counter when my flights are delayed and canceled, making it easier for me to get to my next destination with minimal delays.

On the one hand, this means she often fields calls from me while I am on the road, being forced to find crazy travel solutions that I could never come up with on my own. On the other hand, it also means she is occasionally responsible for little mishaps and unexpected adventures. I love to tease her when things turn out differently than expected.

For example, I once arrived at an airport checkpoint and discovered that everyone seemed to be a little bit too friendly and protective. As I walked through different parts of the terminal and showed my boarding passes, people kept asking me if I needed any help getting to the gate. When I finally did arrive at the gate, the agent looked at me inquisitively and asked, "How did you get here?" Confused, I simply answered that I had walked.

Eventually, I discovered that I had been marked as a blind passenger in the computer. Everywhere I went, people were trying to help me, and were amazed at my uncanny ability to feel my surroundings!

Obviously, my "travel agent" did not do this on purpose. But we had a great laugh over the incident. Most of all, experiences like these make me glad I married someone who shares my twisted sense of humor.

Small Towns and Big Smiles

As a performer, you always dream of showcasing your act in large, prestigious venues. However, some of my best memories are from appearances in small towns and regional festivals, not to mention the other entertainers I have met at these events.

For many years, I performed at Nickel Days, a summer fair held in Thompson, Manitoba. In case you are not already familiar with the geography, it is so far north that the sky does not really get dark at night. Thompson is a small mining town and the kind of place where the population swells once there is something interesting to do, as entire families pour in from the surrounding countryside.

At these kinds of events, performers are treated like royalty. If the locals really like you, at the end of the night they will treat you to a special drink called the "Nickel Belt." This is a tasty mixture served from a 16-inch waterproof rubber mining boot that has been modified with a tap and metal lining to keep the liquid chilled. The actual recipe is a closely guarded secret, and different people seem to make it in unique ways, but my instincts tell me it contains generous proportions of vodka, tequila, beer, and champagne.

The fun thing about fairs is that the grandstand headliners change annually. Over the years, I have opened for Glass Tiger, Kim Mitchell, April Wine, Bobby Vinton, Buddy Knox, and Platinum Blonde. Supporting acts, like me, get to return by popular demand. Performers usually stay in the same hotel, meaning you can rub elbows with big names.

I will never forget opening for Buddy Knox, whose song "Party Doll" topped the charts in 1957. Between sets, he told me wonderful stories of rock 'n' roll tours from days past. On another occasion, I got to open for the legendary band April Wine and their lead singer, Myles Goodwin. I still remember them for being great guys who liked to go golfing during the day before they had to take the stage.

As it turned out, some of the earlier acts had trouble staying on schedule and ran long. When the time came for April Wine to perform, their tour manager insisted that, as headliners, they played at the time they were slotted. So I got bumped to perform after the band, which only provided me with a full arena of eager participants. Or, as I like to remember, there was a night when April Wine opened up for little old me!

The American Comedy Awards

The American Comedy Awards were produced by the legendary *Laugh-In* producer George Schlatter and honored comedy superstars from the stage to film and everywhere in between. As it happened, I was in Los Angeles to do a segment on *The Howie Mandel Show* during the same time as the awards were to be held in 1999.

The event was hosted at the Shrine Auditorium that year. If you recognize the name, it is probably because the venue is famous for being home to numerous awards ceremonies, including the Oscars. I felt compelled to attend... if only I could secure a ticket. Tickets were provided on an invitation-only basis to the elite members of the comedy community.

But, never one to back down from a challenge, I contacted the production company to see if there was even a remote possibility they might let me in. Given that I was performing in comedy clubs around the country and on television, and had relationships with most agents and producers, I thought I might have a chance.

I have called a lot of different companies over the course of my career, so I did not think much about phoning George Schlatter Productions. I got the shock of my life, though, when George himself picked up the line. Here I was, a comedian trying to secure a ticket to an award ceremony, with the award-winning producer of the Grammy Awards, People's Choice Awards, and countless other prestigious programs answering my call!

Between stuttering and stammering while being incredibly star-struck, I introduced myself and asked George if he might be able to grant me access to attend the festivities. He gracefully passed me along to his event coordinator, Jann Rowe, with instructions to fulfill my request. I received credentials for the show that year… and for every year after!

I got to see many of my idols up close that day. Martin Short, dressed as his alter ego, complete with prosthetic body suit outfit, Jimini Glick, was doing impromptu interviews on the red carpet. It was surreal and exciting at the same time. As a kid I watched the Oscars religiously as they were televised from the Shrine Auditorium, and still recall host Whoopi Goldberg telling the world at the end of one of the telecasts that if you dare to dream, you too could be there. That day I was.

I walked the red carpet and rubbed shoulders with people I considered my comedy peers. In one instance I was saying hello to Suzy Soro and Emo Phillips, while in another I was deep in conversation with actor Vincent Schiavelli. As each new celebrity entered the red carpet, a producer called out their name and the paparazzi happily snapped away with their cameras.

The award ceremony was nothing short of magnificent. Steve Martin, Ellen DeGeneres and Richard Pryor were there, as were many of my colleagues. On the way out, everyone received a loot bag with sponsor gifts. One of these gifts served me very well over the years – car battery jumper cables, which served as a wonderful reminder of the awards and a metaphor for my constantly evolving career.

You will not always hear "yes" when you go after what you want, but I can assure you it is always worthwhile to find out, rather than wondering what if!

Memorable Career Moments

Frank Sinatra and I share a birthday, December 12. I sometimes think it is fate that I was born on the same date as Old Blue Eyes, since his signature song, "My Way," is a motto I have lived by for most of my adult life. I have unapologetically dared to dream and push ahead with confidence and bravado, believing in my abilities and taking chances on seemingly impossible goals. As a result, I have performed in some of the coolest places and situations on the planet.

Let me tell you about a few that stand out in my memory...

In 1993, I performed in a minimum-security women's prison outside of Erie, Pennsylvania. I have always been happy to perform anywhere, but this was truly something for the books. The organizers outlined the parameters of what I was and was not allowed to do, and which topics shouldn't be part of the show. My audience was made up of inmates who were not hard-core criminals; most had been convicted of drug offenses, or had been sidekicks to minor crimes.

The experience was novel, even by show business standards. I was frisked and sent through metal detectors prior to my performance. My belongings were scrutinized, and prison guards confiscated my belt, along with some safety pins that were attached to a tag on my dry-cleaned shirt. Eventually, I was led through the living quarters, where I saw that the prisoners' rooms had no doors, and into the auditorium.

The actual performance was wonderful, other than the unnerving feeling that the prison guards were on edge looking for any sudden or unexpected movements.

The whole thing was so unconventional that I made the evening news. A reporter was curious to find out why prisoners were getting entertainment in the first place. I did not have a good answer. I was surprised to learn from the warden that the prisoners had done carwashes and raised funds for a long time to afford my modest fee.

At the other end of the spectrum, as far as government institutions go, I have had the honor of performing at many military bases across Canada and the United States. Soldiers make for fantastic audiences. They work hard and play hard. Best of all, when they are entertained, troops provide hearty laughter as feedback.

Some of my favorite all-time shows in venues took place on military bases, officers clubs, and theaters for soldiers, including:

- The Bob Hope Theatre at Miramar Marine Corps Air Station outside of San Diego. That is where they filmed the movie *Top Gun*, and made the phrase "buzzing the tower" so famous.

- In Fort Knox, Kentucky, at the officers club. Otherwise known as the United States Bullion Depository, it is where the country's gold is stored. I had hoped to see the precious metal for myself, but was informed that the general public is forbidden to come close. What I *did* learn, though, is that the building has impeccable security that includes lasers to ward off any trespassers.

- I also performed at several Canadian military bases, including outposts in Trenton, Meaford, and Gagetown. That deserves a story all onto its own, so I will come back to it later…

I once performed for Roy P. Disney, great-nephew of Walt Disney, at the holiday party for a radio station he owned in Portland, Oregon. The show went so well I got hired to appear again at his house in Toluca Lake for a family party. That, in turn, led to a third booking for another holiday party for Village Roadshow Pictures.

During a radio interview promoting an appearance in Cincinnati, Ohio, the guest following me was Loni Anderson. She was the actress made famous for playing receptionist Jennifer Marlowe on the sitcom *WKRP in Cincinnati.*

As a headliner, you sometimes get VIP treatment, but it would be hard to top the experience I had prior to my performance in Alexandria, Louisiana. My plane was late, touching down right at show time. So the local police chief arranged for an official escort to pick me up from the closest airstrip and blocked every exit on the way to the venue with squad cars. We flew down the highway with sirens blaring. I was still slightly late, but it was certainly a great way to make an entrance.

In the midst of a radio appearance in Dallas, my hypnosis demonstrations were going so well that one call-in guest after another was being blown off to give me more airtime. The producers were ecstatic, certain their ratings were going through the roof with every bit and laugh. One of those callers ended up being Billy Bob Thornton. He was put on hold for such a long time that he finally hung up. That weekend, he went on to win an Oscar.

While performing at Rumors in Winnipeg, Manitoba, the club's owners put me up in the famous Fort Garry Hotel. Local residents claim the place has been haunted ever since a woman committed suicide in room 202 after hearing about the death of her husband. I was unaware of this fact at the time, although my room was on the same floor.

During the week of my appearances, I was having drinks at the hotel bar with my friend, local comedian and television personality Jon Ljungberg. During our chat, he offhandedly asked if I had seen a lady in a gown walking in the hall the night before. I found the question odd, as I *had* followed a woman through the hotel the evening before. She had been alone, seemed to be dressed in a wedding gown, and was carrying her shoes. One does not often see a bride by herself, so the image had stuck in my mind. Having hosted a documentary about the haunting, Jon was very familiar with the story and relevant details, which he took great pleasure in relaying to me. I later inquired with the front desk, but found there were no weddings or bridal parties booked at the hotel for the time that I stayed there.

There are a lot of extraordinary places life will take you if you are just open to following your dreams and seizing opportunities as they arrive. I have gotten to see the world, performed in some wonderful venues, and married a beautiful and caring woman, all because I was always looking for the next chance to experience something amazing. Are you waiting for a sign to move forward with your life, or ready to jump in head-first toward anything the world throws at you?

Bringing People Together

There is nothing quite like performing for a large, appreciative home crowd. That is why I have always loved appearing at the Canadian National Exhibition (or CNE). I grew up going to the famous Toronto fair, and to have been named as a star attraction still gives me a thrill.

CNE has always been a great venue for me. My performance got to be so popular, in fact, that year security had to set up barricades because of the large number of people who were trying to get in to participate. We *literally* stopped traffic in Toronto. But nothing will top the experience I had on Saturday, August 17, 2013, when Darren Chow used my stage for an amazing marriage proposal.

Darren had contacted me previously, letting me know he wanted to surprise his girlfriend, Christine, with an engagement ring. He saw that I was set to perform, and wanted to give his proposal on stage during one of my shows. When I received his email, I responded right away. I was performing in Alaska at the time, but wanted to plan ahead so we could "go big" and make it a truly memorable event. I had a vision for something that required a flawless performance with precision timing.

When the day came, we put our plan into action. We devised a way to ensure that the couple was easy to identify among the thousands of spectators and end up on stage. As part of my act, I mentioned I used to be a skeptic who did not believe in hypnosis, and that if I could find a willing volunteer, I was going to show the crowd that anyone could be hypnotized. That is when I pulled Darren and Christine onto the stage.

In normal conversation, I got them to divulge that they had been dating for six years, and that Darren had not proposed yet. At that point, I told the audience that I was a bit of a troublemaker, and instantly "hypnotized" Darren to pop the question.

But there was a twist! Darren was given a suggestion that he was unable to deliver the lines. After a period of stuttering and fumbling with words, I brought out a large cardboard sign that had been secretly provided to me by the couple's friends. It pronounced: "Christine, will you marry me?" At that point, I allowed Darren to speak the words himself. All at once, the speechless Christine – and the audience of thousands behind us – realized the proposal was not a joke. Christine said, "Yes!" while the audience let out an "aww" at the same time.

As it turns out, making someone pretend to be hypnotized is harder than actually putting them in a trance. In order to prepare for his part, Darren watched online videos of hypnotized subjects to learn how to react. To make his stuttering more convincing, he watched the movie *The King's Speech*.

When it was finished, the surprise proposal made national and international headlines. A video crew from *City TV* captured the moment live, while a reporter from the Toronto Star newspaper was on hand to write about it. I also had my own cameras set up to capture the moment.

The video went viral and has received 150,000 views to date. What the couple probably never knew (until now, if they are reading) is that I also heard from several different media outlets. In fact, the producers for *The Ellen DeGeneres Show* considered offering the couple a wedding on her program, although it did not ultimately materialize.

A Week in the Life of a Performer

I like to tell people I get paid to travel; the performances are just thrown in for free. That usually gets a chuckle, but it is not as far from the truth as you might think. Getting from one place to another is a big part of my life, and it is not always as easy or glamorous as people tend to think.

To give you a sense of how it can be thrilling and grueling at the same time, I recently looked back through my own blog to recall a week of travel that started in Victoria, British Columbia, and ended in Charlottetown, Prince Edward Island. In essence, I crossed from one end of Canada to the other in seven days. My trip included flights, drives, and ferries. As a one-man show, being able to be anywhere on a day's notice is my specialty. That does not necessarily mean it is always easy.

This particular week fell right after Labor Day. It included freshman orientations at universities, along with conferences and fall festivals. It is a great time of year for a performer, because audiences are generally feeling rejuvenated after a summer away from school and possibly a good vacation from work. They have a lot of energy, and bring a sense of excitement to being "back" to whatever they do. That means good moods and enthusiasm, which fuels the laughs and entertainment.

Here are just a few of the adventures I had along the way…

- I forgot my cellphone on a plane, only to have it brought to me by security. I did not realize it was gone until I reached back to turn it on when leaving the terminal. As a side note: Security guards will *not* let you back in to retrieve a lost possession.

- I enjoyed a great meal in Halifax.

- The views of late summer and early fall scenery in New Hampshire were spectacular.

- Next, I performed two shows in one night at different campuses for the University of Toronto.

- I performed at the University of Victoria, which has rabbits all over the campus. I considered bringing one back with me, but changed my mind after thinking about how that might play out with airport security, after the way they had felt about my lost cellphone.

- I had a shuttle driver pick me up at 5 a.m. in a hurry to get to the airport. Speeding along a country road he called "a shortcut," he almost hit a herd of deer that had decided to congregate there in the morning hours.

- I almost missed my next flight because of all the construction going on in Boston, not to mention getting lost and finding myself in gridlock on the I-93 detour.

- After following the wrong set of directions – provided by my laptop computer – I ended up on a ferry, instead of a bridge, trying to get from the mainland to Prince Edward Island.

- I overslept and missed the flight back home because the hotel forgot to give me a wakeup call. But the airline put me on a direct flight instead of a connection, so it worked out. This only happened because someone else had slept through *their* flight, opening up the one available seat for the next two days.

- Someone actually read my contract rider and took it seriously. I usually ask for a new shirt with the venue's logo, so I can remember all the places I have had the pleasure of visiting, along with fruit and veggie platters so I can fuel up in a healthy way before I perform. I also request precise directions to the venue where I will be performing. It is always a delight when these requests are met.

- I got the opportunity to see both the Atlantic and Pacific oceans in the span of one week. I also had the joy of enjoying a surprisingly tasty breakfast of eggs, hash browns, sausage, toast, and jam, with coffee, all for five dollars at the airport on Prince Edward Island.

- And finally, I got back home to unpack and recharge… and noticed I had an upcoming trip to Bermuda to pack for.

The Secret to Seeing the World

Although the big trips to famous destinations undoubtedly stand out in my mind, I have been lucky enough to see many parts of the globe as a traveling performer. The secret to making this work was simple: Wherever I had a chance to appear, I did the best job I possibly could. I also made a concerted effort to remain confident but humble; I always wanted to make an impression on the stage, but never to be a diva behind the scenes.

I knew from my time as a booker that little things like these made a big difference. When audiences were pleased, and industry professionals could tell each other that I was easy to work with, clients who had booked me for one job recommended me for other appearances. By being a solid performer *and* a professional, I could turn one date into several.

Using that approach, for instance, I turned a standing ovation at the Gaylord Opryland resort for the Domino's Pizza national meeting in Nashville into additional bookings with the same company at the Pepsi Center in Ann Arbor, the Fontainebleau Hilton in Miami, and even an appearance at a sales conference in Amsterdam. Each of these provided great joy, and several chances to scratch interesting items off my "bucket list."

None of these adventures would have been possible, though, if I had not made myself into the kind of person others wanted to work with. If you want to see the world, and make it to the top of your field, you can write your own ticket – literally and figuratively – by simply remembering not to make everything about yourself. Help others to get what they want, and they will help advance your career and pull it in the right direction.

Back on TV

If you have been following along, there is one thing you have undoubtedly noticed by now: I do not give up easily. And so, even after a few different starts and stops when it came to my budding television career, I kept plugging forward.

Having found a bit of success on television in the past, I diligently sent more tapes and promotional materials to every show I could think of. I tried *Jenny Jones*, *The Suzanne Somers Show*, and many different incarnations of *The Tonight Show*. I contacted Dennis Miller, Pat Sajak, and Jerry Springer. Throughout this process shows got canceled and producers moved on. But, I kept persevering, and knew that my promotional materials remained in the program's files for possible future segments, even after the faces changed.

Finally, my persistence paid off. One afternoon, my phone sounded with a double ring tone, signifying a long-distance call. My wife answered, but I was immediately leery of what I was hearing. My friend Ofer, a master practical joker, liked to call me (while changing his voice) and claim to be a big-shot television producer. When the man on the other end started speaking, I thought this was another one of his crank calls.

In reality, my caller was John Pascarella, a producer who worked for Maury Povich. He was calling me on behalf of *The Maury Show* because they were putting together a series of episodes that dealt with odd, extreme, and unusual fears or phobias. Once I determined the call was legitimate, I was thrilled to be included – not just because it was another chance to appear on TV, but because I was able to help people who were dealing with serious life problems. And I could show viewers at home that assistance was available to help them overcome their fears, too.

I took the assignment very seriously. In fact, I turned to my friend Robert Doyle, who happens to be a fantastic hypnotist and educator. The past president of a Hypnosis Guild I had connected with several years prior, he helped me brush up on my knowledge of how to deal with phobias. With his assistance, I used an approach called "Fast Phobia Cure" pioneered by Dr. Richard Bandler and Paul McKenna. The basic concept is to mentally take a person before the time they first experienced their phobia, and then to reprogram their subconscious to stay there.

The format for a Maury phobia show was simple: First, guests talked about their fears, which Maury introduced through a slick video package. Then, he discussed with them, on the set, how the fear affected their lives. Following that, guests confronted their phobias when what they were most afraid of was brought out and placed in front of them.

During my appearances, Maury filmed segments on fears of cotton balls, chicken, gum, crabs, flowers, balloons, and roaches. Looking back, I have to admire the way Maury's producers used multiple cameras and crafty editing in a way to capture drama that did not seem so extreme when it was happening live in the studio.

In person, the setup had an almost cartoonish feel. Producers and interns took the stage dressed as chickens, wearing suits made of cotton balls, or carrying mountains of chewed gum on a platter. At this point, some of the show's guests would yell, scream, or cry. A few even ran away, sprinting around the set in a dramatic fashion.

This all made for great television, of course, but there was real mental value in making guests face their fears, as well. There is a psychotherapeutic procedure called "flooding," where the senses are overwhelmed to help with healing. It can be very effective when it comes to treating things like phobias and post-traumatic stress disorder. Using this approach, individuals are exposed to their fears. That stimuli triggers a flight response in the human body, effectively overwhelming the system to the point where a person is suddenly ready to eliminate their fears altogether.

Only after these confrontations had taken place was I introduced. In fact, if you see an episode of the show where I am having an interaction with someone I am about to help, it is likely the first time I have ever met them. Because the episodes are filmed two per day in a before-and-after format, I had time to take the guests to a separate room and spend several hours with them while a different show or segment was being recorded. Then later, we returned to film the conclusion. By then, we were able to show the live studio audience (and viewers at home) that their irrational fears have either disappeared or been drastically diminished.

A question I often get about these shows is: "Were they real or just a setup?" The people I have worked with on *Maury* definitely were *not* actors, just normal people with unusual fears who responded to a television show ad because they wanted help. Or someone they knew had responded to a prompt that went something like: "If you or someone you love has a phobia, call *The Maury Show* now." Producers screened the calls to find the most interesting cases, and then undertook the impossible task of scheduling everyone to be in the same place at the same time. It took a lot of effort on their part – not to mention airfare, wardrobe, props, microphones, and cameras – but the individuals who arrived at the studio in Manhattan were authentic.

The hypnotherapy I used with them is quite real, and I am glad to have been able to provide it. It might have seemed funny to viewers, but thanks to these guests, others who might have been in the same or similar situations found out they were not alone... and that the fears they were holding on to did not have to ruin their lives. Hypnosis is extremely effective in treating fears and phobias, even if it is not always demonstrated on TV in the most conventional way.

From time to time, I come across video clips of these episodes posted on YouTube and other video sharing sites, often with huge numbers of views. When I dip into the comments, I usually observe that they range from "these people are acting" to "I have that fear, too." While I understand the skepticism, it is gratifying for me to think that real people are able to grasp that the help they need is out there if they are willing to go and look for it. While these episodes certainly sensationalized people's problems, they also showed that we all have quirks, and that any fear or phobia can eventually be overcome.

Beyond that, I would be remiss not to point out that Maury Povich is one of the nicest men you could ever meet. In front of the camera, he is a true professional. And behind the scenes, he is always smiling. Every experience I have had with him and his crew has been a blast. They have even given me some of my favorite "people watching" moments. Given that several green rooms are often attached to a common hallway, I sometimes got the chance to overhear guests from other shows arguing about whether a baby *really* looks like a possible father or not.

Aside from the great publicity, my appearances on *The Maury Show* helped to legitimize my ability as a hypnotist. And I got a brand-new title from my work there. Once, when asked what text and graphic I wanted to appear when I came on screen, I replied that the producers should just use my real name, Boris Cherniak. However, they also wanted a title, and "hypnotist" was not enough. Because I had not thought much about the question, I proposed the term "motivational hypnotist," a phrase that had not previously been used anywhere else. I thought it sounded positive and helpful. Later, it helped me transition into the world of corporate motivational speaking, where I combined my hypnosis demonstrations with self-improvement suggestions. It probably was not the only factor that led to those opportunities, but having a new and improved TV title definitely did not hurt.

I Have Got Talent

I have an ongoing relationship with *America's Got Talent*. Although I was invited to audition all the way back in the first season, it was not until the sixth season that I gave it much thought. That was when I received a call from Nigel Caaro, who was serving as the show's senior producer at the time. They were looking for unusual variety acts, and thought I might fit the bill.

This was not the first time this opportunity had come around, and I had always declined on the previous occasions. I knew from experience that my act was difficult to present in 90 seconds, which is all the time you get to showcase your talent. A good hypnosis presentation is a build-up of different comedy routines that require more setup than other types of performances.

Additionally, there are lots of obstacles that come up when working as a hypnotist on TV. First, I have to establish my own credibility – basically, to prove that my participants are not actors, or volunteers who are merely playing along. Then, being the comedy hypnotist that I am, I do not just have to pull subjects into a trance state, but to deliver comedy material at the same time.

That is a lot to accomplish in a minute and a half, even before you take into account things like editing and camera angles, which can fail to capture the nuance of what I do. That is a lot of unknowns, and if some of them do not come together properly, I could fall into the sea of bizarre acts that come off looking ridiculous. As confident as I am in my abilities, I had to seriously ask myself whether the risks are worth it for a resulting 15 minutes of fame.

In the end, though, the challenge proved too tempting. I pride myself on being a leader, and there had never been a hypnotist on the show at the time. I knew everything had to be expertly crafted and executed. Nothing could be taken for granted. One bad appearance could damage my career credibility, and one good performance could raise my profile, so I did not want to take any unnecessary chances.

The first decision I had to make was selecting the best location for an audition. I am a working performer, and the initial audition slots were all being held during my busiest time of the year. One of the only choices that worked for me on my calendar was in Denver. It was only a week away, and there were no flights available on such short notice. After several persistent calls to all the major airlines, I finally found a single seat available on a connection into The Mile High City two days prior to the filming. It was not much, but I felt confident I would be able to work out the audition material and be ready when my chance came.

I should point out that *America's Got Talent* producers only offer a showcase spot. In other words, you are not paid for your audition, and there are no guarantees. In fact, your initial tryout is not even filmed for television. Instead, it is just a chance for you to show off your skills for the producers to help them decide whether you should be allowed to appear in front of the panel of celebrity judges (that is the portion you see on TV).

I arrived early for the audition that morning. I needed to prove to the producers that everything they were seeing was real. That meant hypnotizing my subjects beforehand, testing the depth of their trances, and then tapping into their innate creativity to get the right responses.

Once I checked in, I was identified as a "Q" act. Although that simply meant I was a performer with a preset audition time, in my mind I told myself it stood for "quality." The show's headset-wearing handlers put a wristband on me and gave me a sticker that identified me as a showcasing artist. Soon, I was taken to a conference room with the other "Q" acts. I had brought stage attire along with me and changed in the expansive bathroom. Other performers were also changing, applying makeup, and even singing all around me. Everywhere I looked there was activity and pandemonium. No matter where I turned, there were dozens of other hopefuls trying to create their own big break.

After I passed security and my paperwork was checked, a Q room producer by the name of Shweta Thakur was assigned to me. I was led to believe show assistants would provide me with subjects to hypnotize. However, Shweta informed me that I needed to get these volunteers myself. I was free to pull people from the line of other auditioning acts and their supporters, but the producers could not help in any way. My instincts kicked in, and I went through dozens of men and women calling out for volunteers to be hypnotized. Not many did, and the ones who were willing to step forward had to sign an additional release form that allowed their actions to be filmed.

Still working at a fast pace, I finally got enough subjects together to go back to the Q waiting room and hypnotize my newfound friends. After a few initial assessments, I picked the three who were the strongest subjects and thanked the rest for volunteering before releasing them. We were in such a rush that my subjects and I did not even properly introduce ourselves. I only got to know them by their first names.

My final volunteers ended up being three great visualizers: James, who was part of a musical group; Laura, who was there to support a friend who was auditioning as a female Elvis impersonator; and Shlea, a singer with a great voice who had shortened her name from Ashleigh. I made sure everyone got to their original auditions before mine so that nothing I did interfered with their chances on the show.

The setup for my audition routine was incredibly simple. I was going to send in one of my hypnotized subjects, Shlea, who would believe she was about to perform her own audition for singing. Under my suggestion, she was to seemingly "faint" as if she had become too nervous before ever getting a chance to show off her voice. I would then come into the audition room and present an explanation of what I do, followed by a couple of quick comedy routines using all three of my volunteers.

Everything went according to plan, and Shlea was a fantastic hypnotic subject who responded to my suggestions with precision. At the end, the producer in charge asked if I could duplicate what he had just seen. I replied with an enthusiastic "Yes!"

At that, I was sent to another audition room to wait for a long period of time. My volunteers started getting antsy. They had not eaten all day. In fact, James and his band had driven all night to get to Denver for their audition. As a result, he was fading fast. One of the producers was kind enough to get a couple bags of chips, which gave some momentary relief. As a substitute for a bigger meal and lots of rest, I gave my subjects suggestions of more energy, pulling their minds to a starting point earlier in the day when they had felt more upbeat.

We were finally called in and the same routine was duplicated. After I had finished, I thanked and released my volunteers, taking extreme care to remove the silly suggestions I put in their minds. I was then sent to yet another room to wait for a producer who wanted to ask questions about my background and stage experience. Then, a camera operator named Lindsay took me to a large waiting room and filmed me interacting with other contestants and walking through the crowd.

Finally, my day was done. I was told I had passed through, but that the recordings were being submitted to the network. If I was chosen to appear on air and in front of the panel of celebrity judges, the show would contact me in March. I also had to sign papers promising not to discuss anything that had transpired in the meantime.

The wait was excruciating, and the end result was frustrating. I was not able to appear on the show that year, as my work visa did not meet the necessary parameters. Still, the producers continued to invite me back in the hopes that I might still be able to perform. It never came together and finally, in the 10th season, another hypnotist made it on the air. He put Howie Mandel, a known germaphobe, into a trance and got him to shake hands with the other judges while believing he had tiny rubber gloves protecting him.

When I saw it on air, I tweeted, "Great day for hypnosis. Only wish Howie Mandel got permanent results." I learned later that Howie felt betrayed because his love for the show had been used to ridicule his affliction. I wish I got the opportunity to help him with his phobia in private.

Talented in Canada

Naturally, I was disappointed to have not appeared on *America's Got Talent* (at least not yet). But when I heard a Canadian version of the show was going to be released, I thought it might be the chance I had been waiting for. I went online to register, and after a long wait, received my audition time.

For this attempt to break into the franchise, I wanted to take a different approach. I thought it might be smarter to get producers to take a look at my video first, and then (if I got a chance) come to show them what I could do live after they were already somewhat familiar with my act.

Auditions were held in my home city of Toronto, and I arrived at The Rogers Center early. I had plenty of time to wait, and it seemed most of the city's population did, too – the line was literally hundreds of people long by the time I showed up. People had brought guitars, costumes, and other props.

My initial thoughts, standing outside on the late September morning, were that I hoped it did not begin to rain. After a while, though, I turned my attention to the other prospective contestants. Many were vocalists who were singing their auditions to one another. People impersonating Elvis and Michael Jackson were hanging out in costume, and in character. One girl whose "talent" was to belch on cue was making rude noises a few feet away. Meanwhile, TV cameras were scouting the crowd for interesting acts. I knew from experience they were looking for people they could profile as train wrecks for an early portion of the show.

After I quietly took my place in line, a woman behind me (another singer) recognized me from one of my comedy club shows. I thought that was probably a good sign, and it gave my confidence a bit of a boost. Eventually, I made my way inside, where performers were given wristbands and stadium seats. I was told I only had about 15 minutes before I was taken up to an audition room. I needed to find someone I could hypnotize quickly.

A quick scan revealed several people who are willing to *watch* hypnosis, but only one gentleman who agreed to go into a trance himself. Given that I was under the gun, I quickly started the process of a hypnotic induction. My new friend proved to be a decent candidate, but did not have the kind of explosive personality that is so critical for a successful television appearance.

When the audition came, I used my subject to show a little bit of what I could do. It was not my strongest performance, but it was solid given the restraints of time and the fact that I had exactly one volunteer to choose from. Under the conditions, I knew I had to rely on my reputation, comedic instincts, and a desire by the producers to put something out of the ordinary on the program. Behind me in the hallway were dozens of bands, singers, and magicians, but no other hypnotists.

The producers quizzed me about my act and background, and voiced their concerns about the believability of hypnosis on television. I pointed out that it was easy to set up my act with B-roll that could be provided beforehand. If they showed how I recruited volunteers and hypnotized them, it would make for a great segment – just as it had on the other television shows I had appeared on. I made sure to hand over some DVD footage to support my claims.

In the end, I was given a piece of paper telling me I would be notified in a month if chosen to appear on the program. Unfortunately, I was not contacted. And, even though I thought I might have a good chance at making it in a future season, the program was canceled after its first run.

I still remain hopeful that I will get the chance to show off what I can do on *America's Got Talent* or another program like it. For now, though, I will just have to be satisfied with knowing I gave it a great shot and will keep trying in the future.

Filming Television Pilots

While I have had some successes on television, and a few setbacks, I have always harbored the dream of getting my own television show. In fact, throughout the course of my performing career, I have filmed several different television pilots. Some have involved me as the star of the show, using my talents and persona as the focus; others have had me consulting on projects.

As you may already know, a television pilot is essentially a proof of concept you give to TV networks. It is a sample of a TV show you want to make, showing what the format will be like and how it will be entertaining for viewers. For a lot of the reasons I have already given, hypnosis does not translate perfectly to the screen. People tend to think acting is involved if they cannot see their friends and colleagues being put under a trance under live conditions. Still, there have been a few producers and executives willing to work with me and give it a try.

My first pilot was a show called *Mindjack*, which was being produced by John Feist, whom I had met during my short stint on the show *The Casino*. In addition to that program, he had won an Emmy and People's Choice award for his work on *Survivor,* and had contributed to countless other well-known television programs.

We decided to film *Mindjack* in San Antonio, with the Rivercenter Comedy Club providing space for our casting as well as the club portion of our show. I appeared on *Good Day San Antonio* and requested volunteers. Radio stations publicized the event as well.

Eventually, we settled on Miss Ellie's Pizza Parlor as our main location for hidden camera bits. Two-sided mirror boxes disguised TV equipment so customers who were walking in were not aware of what was going on. I hypnotized volunteers, gave them suggestions, and then released them on unsuspecting bystanders. The reactions from our unscripted, un-hypnotized victims were priceless. They had no idea how to react to seemingly normal people behaving so strangely. All of this was captured on film.

In a frustrating turn of events, *Mindjack* was sold to a network but did not have enough investment to proceed. So we put the idea on hold until a time when all the pieces could come together.

Another pilot, called *Celebrity Crashers*, was filmed with a group of pranksters who got clearances to attend events at the Toronto International Film Festival. Rather than follow the normal set of hidden camera tricks they were already working with, I wanted to push the envelope a little farther. So I hypnotized a volunteer to believe he was a Bollywood celebrity.

I was lucky to have a subject of Indian descent. With a little makeup, some sunglasses, and a bit of stylish wardrobe, he easily passed for Bollywood star Abhishek Bachchan. To help complete the illusion, the producers hired large bodyguards, limousines and expensive cars to arrive in, and a camera crew to follow him around. We made sure red carpets were rolled out everywhere he went. The effect was so genuine that we were able to get our faux entourage through the tightest security details.

The best part was that our hypnotized "celebrity" took his job seriously. He threw fits worthy of the biggest divas, ordering room service and expensive drinks left and right. Fans took notice, mobbing him everywhere he went and asking him for pictures and autographs at every stop.

As much fun as it was, *Celebrity Crashers* did not get picked up by a network. You can bet I will not stop trying, though. Many years ago, my fellow summer campers declared me "Most Likely to Get His Own TV Show." I am going to keep working to prove they were right.

Everything Ends

Occasionally, with my habit of popping up randomly on one side of the world or another, I find the good luck to be near a friend who happens to be in the same place at the same time. There is nothing quite like the pleasure of discovering you can reconnect with an old friend on their home turf, or in a place where you both have some downtime.

Recently, I happened to find myself in Los Angeles on business. As fortune would have it, I was able to arrange a lunch with Howie Mandel and his road manager, Rich Thurber. I was excited to see my fellow Toronto native, and to get some career advice from a seasoned pro who has experienced more success than I have. You should never get to the point where you cannot learn or gain insight from others, and I was eager to get his perspective on what might be next for me.

During our lunch, I mentioned my disappointment that his afternoon talk show had been canceled. I had appeared twice, and loved working with his staff and crew. I had really looked forward to the opportunity to become a regular guest contributor, and to continue with our hidden camera segments that got big laughs with hypnotized subjects. I expected Howie would commiserate, given that it had been his show, and that he had invested so much more time and energy in it than I had.

When I brought it up, though, his response was simple: "Everything ends."

The more I have thought about that answer, the more strongly it has resonated with me. Howie got it, because he had lived through it. From his daytime show to *Deal or No Deal* and *America's Got Talent*, he has had to re-invent himself again and again. Each time, he has come back stronger, to the point where he recently received his own star on the Hollywood Walk of Fame.

The lesson to learn here is to never become complacent. Work your way to the top, and then expect you will have to fight to stay there. I have had to learn and re-learn, to suffer setbacks and change course multiple times. But I have also learned how to take the negative and turn it into a positive. Instead of wasting energy dwelling on what could be, I constantly strive for bigger heights and never despair. Always look ahead and exceed your previous triumphs.

The fact of the matter is that everything ends. But when it does, something even better can begin.

Operation HOT – Honoring Our Troops

Sometimes the cosmos line up to give you a truly special experience. That was certainly the case one morning a few years ago when my phone gave its distinctive two-tone long-distance ring. The caller on the other end of the line identified himself as chef Charles Carroll. I did not know it, but the two of us were about to become friends for life.

He introduced himself with the most passionate delivery I have ever heard. His mission was to take celebrities and entertainers to Afghanistan, bringing them directly to the troops as a thank-you for their service and efforts at building peace around the globe. As luck would have it, a performer had been unable to make the trip as scheduled. And so, after a bit of intensive research, Chief Carroll had decided on me as a replacement.

The performances would be for an international military task force, consisting of soldiers from around the Western world. The team's job was to greet the troops, entertain them, sign autographs, and (hopefully) leave them with lots of memories. It was the type of opportunity I knew came around very rarely.

The departure date for this trip was quickly approaching, and Charles wanted to know if I was willing and available. I answered that I was, even before I had all of the details. I knew right away that this was a fork in the road I had to take. Long ago, my parents had brought me to North America because they wanted a better life for their family. Soldiers like these were helping to make that better life a reality. I have always appreciated those who put their own lives on the line so I could continue to live mine as I please.

In terms of preparation, this gig was distinctly unlike any I have ever worked before. Even though I was not going to be on the front lines, I *was* heading into an area where an active war was taking place. Before I could depart, I had to go through anti-terrorist training and get my doctor to order blood work to check my blood type (in case I happened to need a transfusion while on the trip – military rules). I am happy to report that my blood type is B+. I like to describe it as "B" for Boris, and plus for positive, just like my attitude.

The packing itself was a somewhat nerve-wracking experience. I like to pack and travel light, only having the absolute necessities on hand. Usually, that is not a problem. If I run out of something, I can simply purchase a replacement while I am on the road. However, small luxuries could be invaluable, and irreplaceable, in a place like Afghanistan. I was told to bring a pillow, some suntan lotion, and a pair of shower shoes, along with backups of anything I truly needed. My suitcase was crammed with all the necessities.

Another difference was the level of secrecy involved. Because of the high-profile nature of the mission, and the personalities involved, I was only allowed to divulge to friends and family that I was going to Afghanistan. All other details – including dates, locations, and the identities of other entertainers – had to be kept secret until our return.

Many Cooks in the Kitchen

The inspiration for the trip had come from Charles Carroll himself, and it had taken him more than a year to turn his vision into a reality. In the course of doing some work with a retired general, Charles came up with the idea of feeding the troops an authentic Cajun meal and providing them with a bit of entertainment. It sounded simple enough, but quickly turned into a logistical nightmare.

Even though he enlisted the help of several different celebrity chefs to help with the actual cooking, there were thousands of small details to be arranged. The frozen ingredients to feed five thousand people needed to be shipped by boat to Kuwait, and then transported to Afghanistan from there. All that required approvals from high-ranking officials and coordinated with razor-sharp precision – details that involved dates, times, and menus with military personnel. While all this was going on, he had to raise over $150,000 from private individuals to cover the costs.

In the end, the idea was to put on a morale-boosting show for lots of hard-working soldiers. The troops were going to be provided with a "taste of home" prepared by award-winning chef John Folse. There would also be live cooking demonstrations by acclaimed culinary experts Rick Moonen and Rick Tramonto. Inspirational thank-you messages were recorded to be shown on large screens, with contributions from past presidents and dignitaries as well as Ms. Joanne King Herring, who is depicted in the movie *Charlie Wilson's War*.

As for entertainment, The Three Waiters were there to provide their unique blend of comedy and opera. I contributed a comedy hypnosis show. We had a version of *Jay Leno's Tonight Show* with host and impersonator Marcel Forestieri. He introduced the comedic magician Eric Buss, who yielded the stage for our closing act, an American U2 tribute band called Mysterious Ways.

Getting the Green Light

In the days building up to our departure, the excitement among our group was palpable. Emails flew back and forth in a flurry. Topics ranged from the weather – 92°F and sunny every day – to comical threats by military administrators to make us wear helmets and 30 pounds of gear on stage. Chefs were declaring that they "do not do desserts in the desert" and I assured everyone I was training hard for the mission, "sitting in a sauna, wearing a winter coat with sunglasses, and holding a passport in my hand."

Finally, the day of departure arrived. Because the chefs, entertainers, and film production crew members were all coming from different parts of the continent, we were scheduled to meet at the Dulles airport in Washington, D.C. From there, we were to embark on our flight to Kuwait. After our arrival in the Middle East, we were going to continue our trip on a military transport aircraft to Afghanistan.

Those plans got destroyed when a weather system hit, delaying departing flights for some team members. My flight to Washington from Toronto was delayed by several hours. After numerous phone calls back and forth with the event organizers and various airline booking personnel, I was starting to worry that everything was coming apart. My phone battery was almost exhausted, and the team's travel agent told me not to go anywhere until matters were sorted out. They did not want me arriving in Kuwait on my own, especially if there was not a way to have me catch up with the group later.

Luckily, some last-minute maneuvering made it possible for me to catch a connection to Kuwait going through Frankfurt, bypassing Washington altogether. As a veteran traveler, I knew that it did not help matters if I became agitated. I simply explored my options and let the day run its course. By the time I got on the plane, though, I admit I was exhausted from the anxiety of wondering whether everything was going to work out.

I arrived in Kuwait late in the evening. The process of coming through immigration, and exchanging cash for local currency to purchase a visa, was long and slightly confusing. Eventually, with my papers in order, I was allowed to exit into the terminal. As I walked out of the gates, I suddenly heard a number of women screaming a traditional greeting of excitement in my direction. All I could hear, from every direction, was "lalalala." It took a very startled few seconds for me to realize the greeting was not for me, but for a gentleman in Middle Eastern robes walking behind me.

After a few minutes of searching, it became apparent that not only were those women not at the airport to pick me up, but no one else was, either. Knowing that Kuwait is a deployment area from which soldiers are shipped out to elsewhere in the Middle East, though, I found a dedicated area for new military personnel arrivals. From that waiting area I was able to call my emergency contact, who was aware of the troubles I had with my flights. Given that it was already after 2 a.m., and he was some distance away, he advised me to find a hotel so he could pick me up at 7 o'clock sharp. Rather than spend the $350 I was quoted for half a night of sleep when my body felt like it was noon, I decided to spend a few hours at the airport.

In the morning, I was greeted by a gentleman by the name of Roy Contee. He was not just friendly, but also extremely knowledgeable on local customs. He gave me some tips on Kuwaiti culture, and apologized for the time I spent at the airport. He had not wanted to leave me waiting or cause me any discomfort. Being in a new part of the world, I felt relieved to know we had great people looking out for us, even if we could not always see them in action.

From the airport I was taken to the barracks at Camp Arifjan. The building reminded me very much of a college dorm. I took a quick shower, and intended to walk around outside for a bit. However, instead I decided to take a quick nap to replenish my energy. I was out like a light. It was probably just as well, as my body was playing catch-up, and the temperature outside was 45°C, or around 113°F.

Next Flight to Afghanistan

I might have slept for a whole day, had I not been woken by a phone call advising me to be ready to head to the airport in 10 minutes. I was picked up by Roberta Scheffield and Dennis Woods, a pair I encountered numerous times throughout the journey who handled ground logistics in Kuwait and two of the most amazing people I have come across in my travels. They took great care of us, ensuring we were always comfortable and informed.

They told me that before we could depart for Afghanistan, we had to pick up Jason Zito, who was our sound guru. Being the naturally friendly person I am, I typically call others by their first name. In the military, though, it is more common to use last names only. It did not take long for myself and my colleagues to pick up the habit.

Back at the airport, we waited for Zito by indulging in a little bit of KFC. As you might remember, this happens to be one of my favorite comfort foods. I will admit it was odd enjoying fried chicken halfway across the globe, but that fine meal, and the great company and conversation I got from my new traveling companions, made for a perfect break in the action.

When Zito arrived, it was time to leave the airport. In addition to his bags, he had brought out a guitar that the band required for the show. The guitar had been misdirected and arrived on an earlier flight. Zito was entrusted with picking it up and its safekeeping. Our luggage might have been onerous to carry, had it not been for a gang of blue-suited baggage-handler ninjas that seemed to appear out of nowhere, moving with a coordinated precision. I had been warned about their cold efficiency, but was not ready for their swift appearance. In one second I was talking to Dennis, who was right behind me. In the next moment, I turned around and noticed he had been replaced with a man in blue who was carrying all my bags. If you ever make your way to Kuwait, I encourage you to witness the spectacle for yourself.

From the airport, we departed to Ali Al Salem, a military base in Kuwait. Arriving there was nothing like checking into a commercial flight. On the road to the base, concrete barriers had been set up in a zigzag pattern to discourage terrorist attacks. Before we could actually enter the base, soldiers armed with machine guns, wearing sunglasses and handkerchiefs so as not to be affected by the blowing sand that got everywhere – you could taste the fine grains on your teeth – checked our orders and credentials.

They also inspected our vehicle thoroughly, scouring our luggage and using mirrors attached to long rods to make sure there were no explosives hidden beneath the auto. All of this was done with a deadly sense of seriousness and precision. When we could not find a key to open a guitar case, they considered blowing it up for the sake of safety. After a short, heated back-and-forth conversation, they eventually let it through because our escort was able to vouch for its contents. In that moment, we came perilously close to having no instrument for one of our entertainers to play.

After all of the security measures, we barely had time to make our 3 p.m. flight. When we got there, we discovered that Zito and I were the only civilians coming on board. The rest of the passengers were soldiers heading out on deployment.

Despite the oppressive heat, we were all issued body armor – bulletproof vests and helmets. Together, they did indeed weigh over 30 pounds, making it difficult to move, much less remain comfortable. I suddenly felt that much more appreciative of the sacrifices these troops were making.

Zito is a seasoned traveler. He is constantly on tour with some big band, most recently Backstreet Boys and One Direction. He handles front or back of house sound tech duties and often heads a team of others that provide a great sound experience for the audience. While on the road, he collects hotel room keys as mementos. It was not his first time to a hot part of the world. He does not have to go on stage, and dressing up was not required on this trip. He arrived in shorts.

Military regulations do not allow anyone to board a plane without pants. We were unaware of this regulation. Zito had no pants. I had no extra pants. The person in charge of flights is telling us that we are not getting on the flight in shorts. So our escorts were able to find a ladies' pair of pants in lost and found. The only pair of pants available – a size zero. Zito is a grown man, so size zero only went up to the middle of his thigh. To our amusement, Zito pulled his shorts up above the pants, making his walking restricted, but allowed him to get on the plane. We bonded over the experience, finding humor to defuse the situation at hand. I was marching behind Zito on the way to the bus that took us to the plane, joking, "Today you are low-riding."

We got on the small bus that was to take us to the plane along with the soldiers heading to their deployment mission. I was pushed in first and sat in the back of the bus. Everyone else filed in wearing the heavy protective gear. It was quiet and we sat observing the situation. Someone jumped on the bus and screamed something I could not quite make out. The soldiers next to me started screaming back "One", "Two..." I was observing, unable to comprehend what they were doing. I was the third in line and that was the counting of the number of people on the bus. The soldier on my left shouted, after a short pause that seemed to last a lifetime, "Civi... Three!" and continued the count. I was ousted as a civilian, but included anyway.

Our small bus was otherwise packed with soldiers started to move toward the large military plane resting on the tarmac. It parked just outside the transport and we climbed in through the back of a hollow plane's ramp, open to accept the new arrivals. Next to us, pallets and vehicles were also being loaded next to several rows of seats that had been set up. There were very few windows.

When the aircraft actually took off, it was something of a relief to know we were finally on our way to Afghanistan. With the constant hum of the turbine engines spinning away in the background, I eventually fell asleep. To my surprise, the interior of the aircraft actually became cold in flight.

We arrived at Bagram Airfield in Afghanistan past dark the evening before our scheduled concert. I was assigned a bunk with Eric Buss, who welcomed me to the camp and then promptly went back to sleep. Even with all the jet lag, I was so excited that it was difficult to sleep. Further fueling my adrenaline was the intermittent sounds of jets flying overhead. There were pilots embarking on fresh missions round the clock. I must have eventually gotten some rest, though, because I snored through the night. When Eric confronted me about it in the morning, I immediately answered with "No, YOU snore!" We had a good laugh and instantly bonded over the experience.

Performing for the Troops

We assembled for breakfast and got our briefing about the day's agenda. The stage and band shell were already set up, and a sound and light team from Kuwait was already putting the finishing touches on their AV checks. Seven pallets of gifts for troops were being unpacked and set up for distribution. Swag donated from corporate sponsors was being put on the tables, and our celebrity chefs were busy cooking their meals.

Throughout the day, we were given tours and greeted by high-ranking officers. The experience was invigorating, but also a bit surreal. There we were, in a war-torn territory, trying to help these men and women to forget everything going on around them, if only for an instant. At the same time, it was hard to ignore the fact that everyone had a weapon, and many had two or three, always at the ready. There were machine guns, pistols, and knives everywhere you looked, and they were not for show.

There were signs of the war all around us, too. As we were driven from one place to the next, it was easy to see chains on the side of the road. These chains separated our paths from fields that were littered with broken-down vehicles. Small triangle-shaped signs, hanging from these chains, identified the area beyond our roads as minefields. Once, I saw people actually working in the designated fields. When I inquired why anyone would be out there, our escort explained: "They are contractors defusing the mines."

Still, even with all of this going on, soldiers seemed happy to see us wherever we went. We shook hands and said "thanks" endlessly, meaning it sincerely on each and every occasion.

As the day wore on, a festive mood started to build. The smells from the coming Cajun feast began to swirl in the air, and the band shell was alive with activity. It was a gorgeous day, and soldiers were coming and going as their schedules allowed. There were reportedly 27,000 troops on the base, although many were on peacekeeping missions and were not around to enjoy the meal or entertainment.

When the show started, I was one of the first performers on the bill. My job was to set the tone for the day's events, making people feel lighthearted and fun while taking their minds off the destruction around them. I started by putting on the loudest, brightest shirt I had brought along. It definitely made a strong contrast to the brown and green camouflage all around me, but I wanted to give a sense of silliness that helped everyone relax.

I got off to a great beginning when I was led on stage by a soldier. I will never forget her face. My escort was a tall, pretty girl who seemed very shy. We only had a few minutes to interact, but you could tell she had a contagious smile and a warm personality. I had a hard time thinking that anyone who saw her in another setting would even suspect she knew how to handle a gun.

Once on stage, my first task was to deal with a big obstacle: Everyone around me had a weapon. Being a comedy hypnotist who relies on volunteers, I knew I was going to have a hard time with my show if each hypnotic subject had a large machine gun hanging from their chest. So I decided to begin with the joke. I told the audience that before volunteering they needed to *rock* their weapons. I could see a few confused glances. Then, I looked down at a piece of paper and corrected myself to the proper term... they had to *rack* their weapons for safekeeping next to the stage.

This got hearty laughs, and I had no trouble getting volunteers. From there, my performance came off better than I had ever hoped it might. Laughter filled the auditorium, and even though all of my audience members were standing, they never wavered. They were appreciative and excited, hanging onto the comedic value of every bit and routine.

I had a chance at the end of my act to deliver a personal message of thanks. I pride myself on being a consummate professional, and have developed a skill for holding my composure in any situation through decades of working in front of audiences. On this occasion, though, I found myself feeling overwhelmed with emotion. It was hard to give adequate thanks to those who are putting themselves in harm's way to protect the rest of us. I could tell that many of my fellow entertainers felt the same way when they got their chance to express their gratitude, as well.

With a bit of comedic momentum to push it in the right direction, the rest of the show was a huge hit. Marcel Forestieri, our Jay Leno impersonator, broke the tension with colorful material that hit home and delivered big laughs. Eric Buss provided amazing magic paired with the kind of comedy that left everyone's ribs feeling sore. He finished his time with his signature routine, Spring Snake Symphony, which is performed to the tune of "Blue Danube Waltz" and has been featured on both *Late Night With David Letterman* and *America's Got Talent*.

The Three Waiters have a very unique setup. As trained opera singers, they disguise themselves as members of the audience and then surprise everyone with their vocal abilities. Two of our celebrity chefs, Rick Moonen and Rick Tramonto, had an *Iron Chef*-style competition right on stage. And Mysterious Ways got everybody dancing and singing along to finish the night.

Meeting Your Heroes

I got the opportunity, after my act, to interact with the troops in attendance. It was amazing to see how they lit up, away from the fighting and pressures that came with their daily duties. In that room were some extraordinary people. Many of them told me about their lives, both in Afghanistan and at home, sharing stories and experiences with me that I will never forget. As the evening wore on, I got the chance to laugh and cry with several of them. Looking back, I can only hope I made the same kind of impression on their lives as they have made on mine.

One chance encounter in particular really put everything into perspective for me. One of my on-stage volunteers was a young girl named

Ashleigh whom I saw again during my meet and greet time. We traded stories and she took a few photos with me on her cracked iPhone. She mentioned her birthday was the following month, and she was turning 21. I learned she was a chaplain's assistant. With a few more questions, I found out her job essentially amounted to delivering the news to someone's family after they had died.

I found it difficult to imagine how anyone could undertake such a task, at such a young age, much less to remain so positive through it all. I was truly touched by the strength of her personality, and keep in contact with her through social media to this day.

Our downtime over the next couple of days was like a giant game of show and tell. We visited war rooms and training facilities and were shown military vehicles and weapons. I even got a coin from a general, which is a special tradition that honors the recipient. In the military, coins are handed out to acknowledge appreciation for a job well done. They have imprints on them that indicate units, locations, or even ranks. Sometimes, challenge coins are handed out as part of a handshake, as a secret way to provide a cherished gift. Being "coined" is a great honor, and they are kept like autographs that can be added to a collection of cherished memories and people.

As part of our visitation, our group got to see a couple of secret spaces and facilities that had been pre-screened to remove anything sensitive. One looked exactly like a room I had seen in the movie *War Games*, with large screens, area maps, and computers that could show troop movements. I will never forget the sound of military patrol screaming "red badge" as we passed by to signify visitors who did not have the proper clearance to observe classified information.

In return for all of these tours and adventures, we tried to make sure that the performances never stopped. In quiet moments, or even during our flights, we did our best to entertain the soldiers all around us. We performed skits using intercoms and airplane microphones. We visited cockpits to make sure pilots and airmen got our thanks. We made friends, touched lives, and were humbled by the brave souls who made such a commitment to our safety.

Officers liked to pose challenges to us. They asked Eric, who was a magician, to show them a trick. I was dared to hypnotize subjects on the spot. On one occasion, I can recall having a female soldier become Beyoncé for the amusement of her commanding officer. I also gave a few private sessions for soldiers who wanted to stop smoking.

There was not much of a chance to sleep while we were on the base, but I did not mind. For one thing, I wanted to make as many memories as I could, and to soak in as many details as possible. And I knew many of the troops we were meeting with were sacrificing a lot more than their regular nightly eight hours. If I could have a small opportunity to become a part of their lives and make their days better, I wanted to take it.

As our visit wrapped up, I found it difficult to say goodbye to our new friends. When we first arrived in Afghanistan, you could sense the tension in the air. Everyone we met was ready to fight. When we spoke with soldiers, they answered us in brief, curt tones. By the time we left, though, we could feel everyone's softer sides coming out. You could almost see the appreciation in their eyes.

For people who give so much, our soldiers are not offered our thanks nearly as often as they should be. If I could, I would find everyone who has served bravely, look them in the eyes, shake their hands, and give them a hug. I want them to know I thank them for their sacrifice, their dedication, and for putting their lives on the line for the cause of peace. I only got a glimpse of what that takes, but it was enough to make me appreciate them forever.

The Aftermath

I will be forever thankful to the Operation HOT organizers for having the audacity to come up with a dream, and for including me in the journey. It was an experience like no other that will stay with me forever. My sincerest thanks go out to all of those who planned and executed the impossible, and whose names are too numerous to mention. There were so many people in front of and behind the scenes, whose names I might have forgotten or omitted for space, but whose impact I still feel to this day.

A filmmaker named Christopher Shepard documented our trip from the eyes of a civilian. Several months later, the group reunited in Houston to thank our sponsors and recollect their experiences. Unfortunately, I was on tour at the time and was not able to make the date. However, I sent an emotional video to share my thanks for the experience they had given me, which included photo and video mementos from the trip that I narrated with a poem I wrote:

> *As I sit down to write this, I am saddened to say*
> *That I cannot be in Houston for the celebration today*
> *I am performing on tour, not of duty, but call*
> *And I will have to miss seeing you all.*
>
> *I am filled with emotions from the memories of June*
> *And I hope to say hi to each one of you soon.*
> *From the moment we landed, we got treated like a star*
> *It is not words, but our actions that define who we are.*
>
> *We slept very little and traveled a lot*
> *When we got overseas, we understood why this trip was called HOT.*
> *The troops have responded with laughter and cheer,*
> *They danced into the night… and there was no beer.*
>
> *Words cannot describe the impact we made…*
> *From the words from five presidents to the food the troops ate,*
> *From an impromptu concert at 30,000 feet in the skies*
> *To a smile and a thank-you in just one soldier's eyes.*

Because they do this for freedom, put their lives on the line
So you can live yours and I can live mine.
We made a difference and it changed our lives
How could we ever describe this to our wives?

We drank lots of water, then we went to latrine
and learned a few words that I have never seen
We ate in the mess hall where empty settings remain
We brought love to our heroes by the end of the day.

No challenge would faze us, large tasks felt so small
And if we got stuck, we'd get Chief Longstaff make a call.
He even ordered a volcano and an eclipse for the night
So we could stay longer and miss our next flight.

To Chef Charles, I say "Thank You" for having a dream
And putting together such a wonderful team.
We made a great impact so the troops far away
Could get a taste of home on a hot sunny day.

Special mention goes to sponsors who helped it come true
It was done bigger than ever – big thanks to you.

And to Hilmi, Joe Bendi, Richard, Zito, Wiz and John Huff,
All I have to say to you is "Amazing stuff."
To Patrick and everyone at Mysterious Ways,
You rock my world, I could listen to you play for days.

To my roomie Eric, the three waiters, Brad, John and Russ,
And to our impersonator host Marcel,
I am your biggest fan and have stories to tell.

To Christopher and Jonathan – you captured it all.
Cannot wait to see the documentary in the fall.
To the wonderful chefs – Rick, Fred and the rest.
Your food is amazing and your company best.

To Marty and Lisa, and the team in Kuwait, Dennis, Roberta and Contee
Thanks for getting me to Afghanistan safe.

And if I forgot someone, I really did not
You are always in my heart as part of Operation HOT.

This trip was life-changing with friends that we made
And I am looking forward to our next date.
It is not about money, the glory or fame,
Operation HOT – Let's do it again.

Shortly upon my return home, I received a package that contained a commendation from the city of Houston and a letter from the White House, signed by President Barack Obama, which now hangs proudly in my office wall. There are truly no words to describe the pride and gratitude I feel when I think back to this time in my life.

A Second Deployment

I guess Charles must have heard my plea, because Operation HOT returned in June 2013 to deliver more gifts, food, and performances to troops in Kuwait and Afghanistan. I was thrilled to be invited to be a part of the team again.

The second lineup was similar to the first, but with even more big names. The roster included coach Lou Holtz of Notre Dame fame, Chef Robert Irvine from *Dinner: Impossible*, *Iron Chef*, and *Worst Cooks in America*, Secret Millionaire Steve Kaplan, and Laura McIntosh of *Bringing*

It Home. Comedian Carmen Barton and I were on hand to provide laughs, and a different U2 tribute band called L.A.vation provided the music. We were backed by a large light and sound team from Kuwait, a video crew, and our military liaison, Chief David Longstaff.

For the second tour, the grand show was held in Kandahar, Afghanistan. We also traveled by helicopter to numerous forward operating bases to provide entertainment inspiration in remote locations.

Once again, the event was a big hit. Chef Charles mixed together a team of personalities and entertainers with the same care and creativity he might use to create a four-star meal. Coach Lou was a tough cookie who brought a bag of challenge coins with him everywhere he went. He refused to drink anything but Diet Coke. We worried that might be a problem, in the intense heat, but he never wavered or gave into drinking water.

Robert Irvine and his team went to work giving dazzling food demonstrations. Carmen, always dressed immaculately like a glamour girl, made everyone laugh and gawk both on stage and off. Steve Kaplan delivered inspirational speeches and financial wisdom while providing books donated by his publisher. Laura McIntosh was everywhere, making sure the story of our trip was captured on film while reporting on everything that transpired. L.A.vation brought the music and energy of the world's biggest band, making you feel as if you'd stepped directly into a U2 concert, even if it was just a makeshift sing-along.

In Kandahar, everything was set for our main show. The staging gear had been prepared the night before, so we performed our sound checks and retreated for meet and greet time, along with some much-needed sleep. However, during the night, strong winds blew over the stage setup, breaking one of the large LCD screens and putting everything else in disarray. To my amazement, the crew proceeded to rearrange the show gear as if nothing had happened, resetting everything to the point that it felt like there had not been any setbacks at all. It is amazing to see what can happen when true professionals are so dedicated to their work.

The troops came in droves, and the performance had elements of both fun and inspiration. We were excited to be there, and our audience seemed equally enthusiastic. Once again, we followed our performance by signing autographs, hugging servicemen and women, and expressing our appreciation for their work.

The tour was a busy one. We normally visited two forward operating bases per day and stopped wherever possible for meet and greets. Some of our shows were impromptu, and delivered without microphones or sound systems. In between appearances, we visited hospitals and performed for small groups. Often, I saw band members playing with makeshift instruments because they were not able to bring equipment along from one camp to another. Guitars were borrowed from soldiers who had them on base, and drums were replaced by used pots and pans as the drummer banged on them with kitchen utensils while sitting on a bucket. We simply made do with what we had, and had a great time in the process.

When moving from one location to the next, we wore protective gear that just intensified the scorching heat outdoors. At one point, I was told the thermometer read 162°F on the tarmac. That seemed hotter than anything imaginable, until I stepped closer to the helicopter we were about to board and felt the exhaust coming from the engines.

Each of the bases we visited had names, although I was not always able to take note of them at the time. Occasionally, soldiers we traveled with offered bits of geographical trivia. For example, they might say, "Over there is the Pakistani border," or give other general pointers.

For the second time, I found it difficult to say goodbye and let go. There are still so many faces and memories of that tour that I cherish to this day. It has truly been one of my biggest honors.

Upon returning to Kuwait, our group had time to reflect on our trip. We also filmed a short video where each of us got to walk on screen while Robert Irvine discussed the journey. At the end of the clip, Chef Charles was invited to hold the Operation HOT sign while our mischievous bunch dumped water on him (similar to the way players dump Gatorade on coaches at the end of the championship). In the hot temperatures, the liquid dried almost instantly. But we were all still overjoyed from what had been accomplished, so everyone was happy to be delightfully splashed. Just as we had in Afghanistan, we made happiness out of what was on hand.

Luckily, I was able to attend the second reunion and receive another letter from the White House. While having a piece of paper signed by the leader of the free world is a testimonial like none other, it is really the memories I think of most, and that I am most grateful for, when I see that presidential seal on my wall. Operation HOT was exhausting, but it was also an exhilarating experience I would not have traded for anything.

You Can Do Anything!

So much of life is about proximity. There is proximity to fame, proximity to wealth, proximity to power and proximity to opportunity. A lot of people think you have to be born near them to take advantage of the situation, but that is not necessarily true. Opportunity – which leads to wealth, fame, and success – can come without any warning or notice. You simply have to be ready to recognize the clues, so you can act at the right time.

In 2014 I joined an elite group of inspirational TED speakers. TED is a series of nonprofit presentations that focus on areas where Technology, Entertainment, and Design are converging and changing our world. They are meant to highlight interesting topics in an informative and inspiring way.

I was incredibly flattered to be offered such an honor, and knew almost right away what I wanted to talk about. I chose the title "Prophetic Thinking." That is a term I invented, and I think it perfectly encapsulates the concept of seizing the moment and looking for the opportunities that are all around. Naturally, I made hypnosis the centerpiece of my talk, using it to illustrate the hidden control our thoughts exert over our everyday habits and actions.

The event itself was hosted and filmed at the Ontario Science Center in Toronto on November 15, 2014. I love being able to share wonderful moments of my life with the people that matter most to me, so I took my youngest daughter along to the presentation. The other speakers, which included Olympic athletes, business tycoons, and activists, were exhilarating. I hoped to deliver as much of an impact as they did, and my speech was very well-received, both in person and online.

You can view my TED talk by visiting the project's website and searching for "hypnotist The Incredible Boris." That moment did not just give me a chance to share my point of view with some young people who are watching, but it also inspired me to write this book and share my story with the world. I hope you have found it helpful.

If the decision to write the book was easy, the execution was not. Putting my thoughts into written form meant undergoing a huge challenge. Countless hours were spent trying to remember names, faces, and details, and countless more were devoted to figuring out what I could or should include in these pages and which topics were better left out.

One of the hardest things about this whole process was deciding when and where the book should end. There have been a lot of highs and lows in my life so far, and if history is any guide, there are many more still to come. How would I feel if I typed "The End" and found another new adventure was just around the corner? The book cannot go on forever, but how would I know when it was truly complete?

Ultimately, what pushed me to move forward was not the idea that there are not more chapters to my story, but that I have a message I want to put into the world that just cannot wait. That message is a simple one, and it is something I live and exemplify every day: *You can do anything!*

That is not just a slogan; it is my deepest belief and the foundation of every shred of success that has come my way. It is also the one message I want you to be sure you take with you when you hear me speak or read my words. And so, before you finish with this book and go back to the rest of your life, I want to spend a few pages explaining what that means, and how you can use it to find your own success and become the headliner you were meant to be in your life or career.

Alien of Extraordinary Abilities

At some point, the U.S. government decided that my appearances on television, and at festivals, corporate meetings, and comedy clubs all added up to a certain amount of credibility. And so, they changed my work visa to categorize me as an "Alien of Extraordinary Abilities," a specialized title that allows unrestricted international work travel. It is typically reserved for Oscar winners and those who receive international awards. I consider that designation to be as valuable as any of the other honors I have received.

And truth be told, I *do* feel like I have an extraordinary ability… it just probably is not what you think. My big talent is not that I have the world's sharpest comedic instincts, or some sort of supernatural power to control minds. Instead, my "special ability" has always been to find my dream, chase it, and never give up.

I come from very meager beginnings. My parents arrived in Canada with only $200 and the clothes we were wearing. As a child, I often wore shoes and jeans that had been donated to the needy. I did not have much, but I knew from an early age that I loved to make people laugh. So I cultivated that talent as best as I could.

Money was never my big motivation. I always wanted to value myself on the success of my performances, and to chase new and exciting opportunities that came along. There were financial rewards, of course, but those were a direct result of pursuing my passion every day instead of giving up or taking the safe path. There is an old saying that remains entirely true: If you find a profession you love, you will never have to work a day in your life.

Because I devoted myself to my art, I naturally got better and better at it. As I moved through my career, the venues got bigger and classier, and my audiences grew. I started at small clubs and worked my way up to big casinos, international festivals, and even TV studios. And at every step, I kept my focus on being clean and positive, and entertaining others. I stayed true to myself, and the people who promoted and booked performers started to notice.

Reaching any dream takes a consistent effort. That is true whether you want to become a comedy hypnotist or any other profession. I have seen numerous examples of this in my own career. A performer's life is full of incredible highs and extreme lows. Nearly every day you are faced with someone who is either giving you lots of praise for a successful performance or turning you down because they do not feel your act is suitable for their function. All of this is on top of the normal trials and tribulations that come with being a living and breathing human being.

Regardless of the outcome of any particular appearance or interaction, or the way your day might happen to be going, you have to entertain audiences and pay your bills. You are constantly reminded that "you are only as good as your last show," because the next one might be difficult to find. If you want to keep moving up, you have to keep innovating, experimenting, and finding new ways of doing things.

When people see me perform now, they feel like they are being entertained or educated for a set amount of time, and that is certainly true. What they are also witnessing, though, is the result of decades of work. They do not necessarily recognize that I had to be so persistent in my approach to show business. It is what got me to where I am today.

Think long and hard about which goals in your life really motivate you to work. What could you become that inspires you to new heights? Once you have identified that goal, do not let anything stand in the way of achieving it. There are certainly going to be setbacks, and highs and lows are part of the journey. If you never give up, though, you will always be moving closer and closer to your dream.

Follow Your Dreams

In this book, I have tried to be strikingly honest about where I have come from and how I have made it in show business. I have also tried to be very transparent about the fact that I am not successful in everything I take on. In fact, I can go as far as to say that the majority of my projects and attempts are *unsuccessful*. I simply accept that as the price of ambition. Sometimes, you can do a hundred things that do not work out before you find one that does.

A lot of getting ahead in life, and in any career, is simply a matter of getting through those hundred or so negative responses to find a successful outcome. I can tell you firsthand as an entertainer that talent is not enough. You can send dozens and dozens of kits to dozens and dozens of producers, for years, before you appear on television. But once you do, your profile goes to a whole new level and you are suddenly set apart from the rest.

In working with executives and top achievers around the world, I have found that the same thing occurs in virtually every field. You have to stay persistent, learn from your mistakes, and continually fine-tune your approach if you want to get the right outcomes. By constantly visualizing a positive scenario, you can drive yourself to succeed through sheer determination. The law of averages dictates that if you spend enough time trying, you *will* eventually succeed. The way to set yourself apart in the crowd is through effort and perseverance.

Also, you cannot be afraid to do things your own way. Being passionate, and different, are advantages even when they do not seem like it.

Consider the world of fast food. Nearly every restaurant in the world serves a round hamburger on a round bun. At one point, the folks at Wendy's decided they wanted to, quite literally, be a square peg in a round market. By using square pieces of fresh beef, instead of round burgers that had been frozen like everyone else, they were able to stand out and establish themselves. Now, they sell millions and millions of these sandwiches every month.

I took a similar approach to my performing career. Instead of being like everyone else, I focused on the qualities and attitudes that set me apart. Some of it was unconventional, but it also made it easier for audiences and bookers to tell what made me different. I might not know you personally, but I know there is something that sets you apart from everyone else who is chasing your dream, too. Embrace that, and make it a part of your identity. It just might be what drives you forward to success.

There are going to be some people who will doubt and discourage you along the way. That is fine. You do not have to listen to them. In fact, every time someone tells you that you can't, I want you to remember that *Boris says you can.*

I am living proof that you can reach your dreams, regardless of where you come from or what you are hoping to accomplish. It could have been easy to accept that I was a small immigrant from a foreign land and blend into the crowd. Instead, I changed my self-talk to become a giant in the world of show business and put myself on stage. Keep pushing through to achieve your vision and you can do the same, even if your end goal looks a lot different from mine.

I love my job. I get paid to travel the world and to make people laugh. I found a career that makes me feel passionate enough that I want to leap out of bed in the morning. I have gotten to travel all over the globe, perform for royalty, and meet lots of incredibly interesting people.

My favorite thing about all of this, though, is not the money, the cheering crowds, or even the stories – it is the smile I can put on your face. When I look into an audience and see the sparkle in your eyes as you forget all the troubles that were with you when you stepped into the theater, that is my magic moment.

This book, my story, and my life are devoted to inspiring you. I want you to dare to achieve something that seems utterly impossible. And when you finally do achieve it, I want you to feel the same joy I do.

Whether you picked up this book because you saw one of my shows or speeches, or stumbled onto this book knowing nothing about me, I hope you will gain a bigger vision for the life that is ahead of you. I want to thank you for giving me a chance to share what I have learned, and to wish you every success in the world.

My TED talk inspired me to tell my story and write this book. I hope it inspires you to achieve whatever you desire. I can do anything, and so can YOU.

Acknowledgments

I would like to thank the many people in my life who shaped the words on these pages and gave me a reason to write this book. As I was writing, I was reliving the memories that sparked years of passion and turmoil. I owe my gratitude to everyone who was instrumental in the creation of the person I have become today and the message I impart on everyone I meet.

Thanks to the tireless editors, proofreaders, fact checkers and designers: Dr. Judy Hagshi, who read the first manuscript and provided questions and ideas to make the words jump out of the page, Robert Doyle for his guidance and friendship, Anthony Galie for his friendship and mentorship, and Matt Sherwood for taking my words and arranging them in a manner so my message was heard loud and clear. I also want to thank the people in my life who helped me laugh through it all, and gave me the friendships I hold so dear – the comedians, fans, teachers, hypnotists, bookers, agents, managers, and publicists. Some recognized my passion and determination to succeed, while others failed to see my vision and only fueled the drive.

Thank you to Ofer Krausz for being my close friend from the time we were teenagers, and for providing laughter and keeping me grounded, no matter what the distance, while always giving useful advice. Most of all, I want to thank my family for giving me love and enduring the hardships by my side, all while seeing the passion that drives me. My parents, who were supportive and believed in me when my career was only a dream, and for all the sacrifices they made so their children could have a better life. My wife, who is always my voice of reason, who used the words "I can do anything" as the message to instill in our kids and makes every obstacle just a hurdle. To my kids, life is simply what you leave behind, and you are my proudest accomplishments.

I can't wait to see what the next chapter brings.

About the Author

Boris Cherniak is an engaging motivational speaker, comedian, and amazing hypnotist. He is an exciting event entertainer that draws from a vast entertainment career to empower, inspire, and deliver an unforgettable experience.

Boris is a TED speaker and a frequent guest on national television. During his career that spans more than three decades, Boris has traveled extensively and appeared alongside some of the most enigmatic world leaders, which include royalty, athletes, Hollywood celebrities, and esteemed educators.

He was twice named Canadian Special Events Entertainer of the Year, is a recipient of two Global Leader awards, and has received commendations from the White House and the City of Houston. His presentations are lighthearted and deliver the message of positive thinking loud and clear.

Boris lives in Toronto with his wife, Daphna, and daughters Sophia and Julia. They have no pets yet, but the kids keep asking for a bunny.

To learn more, or to book Boris for an appearance, visit **incredibleboris.com.**

Made in the USA
Middletown, DE
03 October 2022

11605830R00139